The Loving Yourself Workbook for Girls:

How to Get to Know Yourself, Pump Up Your Confidence, and Feel Good Being You

Diana Rachel Bletter

Copyright © Kent & Cordell, POB 808, Westhampton Beach, NY 11978

Edited by Kristy Phillips

Cover Illustration and Design by Cait Brennan

Interior Illustrations by Derin Kumbasar

ISBN: 978-0-9853432-7-9 (PAPERBACK)

Foreword

For Parents, Practitioners, and Adults Who Care About Girls

by Dr. Paula

As a board-certified pediatrician, I have spent 44 years taking care of children of all ages. For the past 18 years, I have focused on working with preteen and female adolescents.

So, when I was asked to write the foreword to *The Loving Yourself Workbook for Girls,* I leapt at the opportunity. This population presents the greatest challenges. I have treated girls who suffer from multiple complaints including chronic stomach pain, headaches, fatigue, poor nutrition and an inability to concentrate and stay focused even on tasks that were truly important to them.

That's why *The Loving Workbook for Girls* is desperately needed. It comes at the perfect time to help girls deal with their life challenges. This book is an empowering guide, whether for girls who live in extreme poverty and family distress, or those who have strong levels of family support and economic well-being.

The author provides guidance that any young person can relate to. Each of the ten chapters offers support and suggestions. There are activities that girls can do, and questions for them to answer to get to know themselves better. The book serves as a tool to help girls sort through a variety of challenges, including strengthening their body image, making friends, confronting bullies, dealing with their emotions, and handling social media.

I have watched practitioners as well as parents from all walks of life struggle to find a way to help. This book is an invaluable resource that can be used to guide pre-teen and adolescent females, written with compassion in a language they understand.

Girls will receive vital messages about self-awareness, self-confidence and learning to love who they are. Within these pages are comfort, clarity, and wisdom.

—Dr. Paula M. Elbirt, MD, Specializing in Adolescent Medicine

Before You Begin Your Loving Yourself Workbook . . .

I want to tell you that I believe in creating a safe and inclusive space for all readers. I've done my best to make this book as diverse and inclusive as possible, celebrating the beautiful tapestry of all girls of so many wonderful different races, sizes, genders, capabilities, beliefs, and backgrounds.

I understand that each girl's journey is unique. Your definition of what it means to be a girl is also very personal. You might not even choose to call yourself a girl! At times, you might feel you're a girl, and then you might feel like a boy, a combination of both, or something else. I'm using the word *girls,* as well as *she* and *her,* to keep the book as simple and clear as possible. Even if you aren't sure you want to be labeled as a girl, the information in this book will help you start off on your adventure of loving yourself. If you're reading this book to yourself or out loud, you can choose another pronoun or word if that makes you more comfortable. And if you're exploring your gender and what that means for you, take a look at some of the resources at the end of the book.

Whatever your challenges, I urge you to find a trusted adult to speak to, and try your best to share your feelings and thoughts. The world can be a scary place but there are people to guide you. Look around. Maybe you can talk to your pediatrician, school nurse or family doctor. You are not alone, even if you feel like you are. You can find help.

I offer you my words to help you feel that you're the best **you** you can be. I hope to guide you on your journey to loving yourself. I know these pages will provide you with important knowledge and offer support so you can love yourself more and more. You can already start this adventure today. You can start right now!

I kindly ask you to leave a review of **The Loving Yourself Workbook for Girls** on Amazon at https://www.azonlinks.com/B0CRB2TQF2. Your feedback is invaluable and helps me improve my work and reach more readers who might benefit from its uplifting messages. When you share your thoughts through a review, you not only encourage me in my work, but you also help others discover the book.

Additionally, I encourage you to share this book with your friends and family. By spreading the message of self-love and empowerment, we can create a ripple effect of positivity and inspire others to embrace their unique selves. Share this book with health-care providers, pediatricians and family doctors.

Part of the book's proceeds go to supporting ELEM, an organization that offers inclusive, innovative programs to help at-risk girls: https://elem.org.

With love and gratitude,

Diana

For all my wonderful children and for every girl reading this book

CONTENTS

Introduction 9

01 - Get to Know Yourself 23

02 - Take Care of Yourself 45

03 - Take Care of All of You 63

04 - Loving Your Body 91

05 - How to Make Friends—and Be a Better Friend 117

06 - Feel All Your Feelings 135

07 - Don't Let Fear Stop You 157

08 - Pump up Your Confidence 171

09 - Social Media Is Tricky 187

10 - Make the World a Better Place 195

A Few Last Words 199

References & Resources: Where to Turn When You've Finished This Book 203

About the Author 206

Introduction

Way to go! If you're reading this book on your own—or with a friend or trusted adult—then you're about to begin the greatest adventure of your life! You're going to embark on a special trip to get to know yourself and love yourself. You'll begin to celebrate all that you are.

According to the United Nations, there are about 900,000,000 girls and young women in the world. But if you traveled all around the Earth, you'd never meet anyone just like you! From the top of your head down to your toes, you're unique, special, and one of a kind. There's only one YOU on the planet. And you'll never find anyone who deserves your love as much as you.

On the day you were born, *you* were born to be *you,* and nobody else. Inside you is an unusual spark that helps light up the world. And once you feel more love for yourself, you'll learn how to make that spark turn into a bright flame.

This book is like an exciting expedition to discover just how strong, brave, smart—and, yes, fun—you are! This isn't an ordinary book, but a chance to set out to discover who you are and what makes you special.

You'll discover what makes you tick inside and out. You're going to explore your likes and dislikes, your inner and outer world, and the changes going on inside your body, heart, mind, and soul. Just like in a fairy tale, where a hero has to slay dragons, you're going to learn how to act like a hero and do things you're sometimes afraid to do.

Now, you might already be rolling your eyes. You probably also have a lot of questions. You might wonder:

- How exactly can I do things that really scare me?
- How can I boost my self-confidence?
- How can I build a positive body image, changing how I feel about the way I look?
- How can I learn to feel unique being me?
- How can I make and keep friends?
- How can I face the challenges of being a girl, whatever that means to me?
- What can I do to love myself?

With all these questions, you might not be sure you're going to get the answers. You will though. This book is filled with tools and tips to help guide you.

I wish I'd had a book like this when I was your age. I had no self-confidence–as in zip, zero–and I worried how I'd face life's challenges. I didn't know what it meant to be a girl, and I struggled with my body image. All in all, I simply didn't know how to love myself.

That's why I decided to write this book. I want to help you discover and love who you are.

You might be curious about who I am. And since I'm writing this book, let me tell you a few things about me:

I once played Peter Pan in a play at day camp. I danced and sang "I Won't Grow Up." Why would anyone want to grow up? It seemed so boring! I did grow up (we all have to—it's part of life, isn't it?), but I've kept my vow. I'm one of those grown-ups who never forgot they were once a kid. I still love to climb trees, ride my bicycle without hands, run, skip, snowboard, play with kids, and make silly faces.

I saved all the patches I earned from my Girl Scout troop and sewed them onto my denim jacket, which I love to wear.

I learned how to make granola when I was about your age, and I still make it.

I love the colors turquoise and indigo, mostly because the names are fancy, like croissants.

I like collecting seashells, feathers, and smooth stones.

I have four children, two stepchildren, and an unofficially adopted daughter from Ethiopia.

As you can see, I love kids. I love talking to kids, and, more importantly, I love listening to them. I listen to what kids are going through, and I understand how life is sometimes simply hard and full of challenges. Life can be very tough! I've learned a lot over the years, and this book is a compilation (like a collection) of things I now understand that can guide you.

Loving yourself isn't always easy. Did you know that the problems of self-hatred and depression are quite common among girls? While women have opened many doors in politics, sports, and sciences, girls still struggle to accept themselves.

The Centers for Disease Control and Prevention did a study of hospital emergency departments around the United

States. The study discovered a terrible fact: girls aged ten to fourteen are harming themselves almost three times more often than they did in 2009!

How could this be? There are many reasons that could explain the increase in the number of girls who hurt themselves. One explanation might be that some girls feel peer pressure. They might think they aren't "good enough." There are girls who might suffer from depression, anxiety, or emotional pain. And perhaps, too, they haven't yet learned how to love themselves. Because if you love yourself, you wouldn't hurt yourself. You would treat yourself like a precious gem. You would try to *polish* yourself, not *punish* yourself.

Learning to love yourself is the most important thing you can do in your life. It will make you feel stronger, healthier, and happier. Once you feel more love for yourself, everything in your life will get better.

Loving yourself will help you:

- Make good choices
- Take care of yourself
- Pump up your self-esteem
- Find more courage
- Learn more acceptance
- Improve your friendships and relationships with your family

And it's not only that! Once you start on the adventure of self-love, it will make it easier for you to:

- Say no to others so you can say yes to yourself
- Treat yourself with kindness, the way you treat your best friend
- Be in a crowd of kids and not feel the need to compete or compare yourself to others
- Know what you like and what you don't like
- Feel okay being you, even when life sometimes gets tough

This book is divided into ten chapters.

In Chapter 1, you'll learn how to get to know yourself, and then you'll start to understand what makes you special and unique. Chapters 2 and 3 are about how to take care of yourself and be nice to yourself each day. Chapter 4 is about your body. Chapter 5 talks about how to find friends and be a better friend.

In Chapters 6 through 8, you'll learn about how to embrace your feelings, push past your fear, and pump up your confidence. Social media is the topic of Chapter 9. And Chapter 10 is about how you can make the world a better place.

Finally, you'll learn ten important ways to feel good about yourself, and each day, you'll see how you can be a role model for self-love. You'll also be able to make a positive impact on others, passing on the message of how important it is to love yourself.

Important Note:

To get the most out of this book, keep a pen or pencil nearby so you can write things down as you read, answer the questions, and do some of the fun activities. These pages are in black-and-white so that you can add your own colors and creativity. You can decorate this book with markers, stickers, highlights and glitter to make it your own.

You go to school to learn important subjects, but learning to love yourself is THE most important subject you need to learn. You'll be you your whole life, and now's the time to learn to love the incredible girl you are.

The Loving Yourself Quiz

You're about to take your first step on your trip toward self-love, and there's no right or wrong time to begin. You're exactly where you're supposed to be to start!

So, before you begin, here are some yes-or-no questions for you to answer. By the end of this book, you can answer the same questions again to see the progress you've made. Please don't use your answers to this quiz as a reason to get upset with yourself. These questions are part of your new way of seeing yourself. They're meant to give you new awareness. You're about to change how you feel about yourself. How cool is that?

Here we go:

- Do you have a lot of self-doubt?____________________
- Do you struggle with body image issues?________________
- Do you often feel bad about who you are?_______________
- Are you mean to yourself?_________________________
- Do you fear other kids won't like you when they find out who you really are?_________________________
- Are you afraid of failing and not living up to expectations?___________________________________
- Do you have a hard time making decisions because you're scared other people won't like you?_______________
- Is it hard for you to experience all your feelings?

  ____

- Do you get really angry at yourself for making mistakes? ____________________
- Do you have a hard time just being you? ____________________

When I was your age, I answered yes to *all* these questions. I was so afraid of not being perfect. I really didn't like myself, and I thought that if people really knew me, they wouldn't like me either.

So, don't be worried if you answered yes to all the questions. The good news is that you're reading this book and you're ready to change. That's the magic of learning to love yourself.

"Pledge that you'll look in the mirror and find the unique beauty in you."

TYRA BANKS

Write a Letter to Yourself from Yourself: And Say ONLY Positive Things

Pretend it's Friendship Day, which is celebrated on July 30 around the world. Write a letter *to* yourself *from* yourself, as your very best friend.

This doesn't mean you don't have another BFF. It just means that it's important to be your own best friend. You're with yourself all the time, so you need to talk to yourself nicely, compliment yourself, and have fun in your own presence!

Before you read this book any further, please stop for a few moments and decide to write yourself a Friendship Day card. At first, you might feel silly, weird, nerdy, or completely clueless, but just reading your own words will give you power.

Pick somewhere special. Or somewhere ordinary. You can be inside your bedroom or by a big tree in a park. Wear clothes that make you feel cozy and good about yourself. Then write down a few things about yourself that you like.

Here are a few examples. The first is my own!

"Dear Dean [one of my favorite nicknames], as your BFF, I have to say that I think you're SO cool. Even when you make mistakes and get things wrong, you keep trying. You never give up! You're unique. You try to be nice to everyone—even people who aren't nice to you! I love your hazel eyes and your funny-looking toes and your freckles. I love, love, LOVE you!"

Here's another example:

"I'm so happy to be your BFF. I promise to always believe in you. I promise I won't be hard on you. I promise that even if other people are upset with or mean to you, I'll always be kind to you. XOX."

And one more:

"I love your funny laugh and style in clothes. I love the color of your hair. I love it when you eat an ice cream cone and some ice cream gets on the tip of your nose! I just love you!"

Go on. Don't be shy. Take a few moments to write this letter to yourself.

LETTER TO YOURSELF FROM YOURSELF

Now that you're done, read it out loud for your ears alone. Then cross your arms over your chest and give yourself a hug. A really big hug.

Hold it for a while so you take in that swoosh of love.

Hugs are the best. And now you're ready for the next step.

Find a piece of jewelry that will serve as a reminder that you're embarking on this self-love adventure. I wear one of my mother's rings (she passed away a while ago), and during bad times, I can look down on it and feel her strength and love.

You can buy yourself an anklet or necklace or pierce your ears. You don't have to wait for Christmas or your birthday. Do you have a half-birthday coming up? You can buy yourself a little gift as a celebration of who you are and how much you want to start loving being YOU.

This self-love is like a stone that's dropped into a lake and keeps sending out ripples. Once you love yourself, more and more love will keep spreading to fill up the entire world.

After you read the letter, put it somewhere safe. Every time you're feeling bad about yourself, you can take out the letter and reread it as a reminder of how amazingly awesome you are.

Remember! If you don't love yourself completely, it really doesn't matter how many times people say they love you because you won't feel it deep within. And if you don't love and accept yourself, it's hard to love and accept other people.

Self-love also works as an invisible weapon. You'll start to feel a bit like Wonder Woman with a protective shield around you. It won't hurt as much when someone says something mean to you or stops being your friend. When you have love for yourself, you can face anything in life!

And now, put on your imaginary backpack and hiking boots, get into your sparkly purple jeep, and start on your loving-yourself safari!

01

Get to Know Yourself

"The question isn't who is going to let me—it's who is going to stop me?"

— AYN RAND

Just about every day, you can see yourself in the mirror. But do you really know the person staring back at you? In this chapter, you're going to start getting to know yourself and who you really are.

Do you have that pen and paper still handy? If not, go grab them, because it's time to get to know yourself, and using a pen and paper is the best way to do that. In fact, scientists say there's a flow of energy that connects your brain to your hand when you write. So, let's go.

Your Name

The most important sound in the world is your name. It's what you heard as a baby. It's your identity.

What's your name?--

Many names have meanings. For example, Shayna means beautiful in Yiddish. Stella is from the Greek word for a star. You might have been named after someone in your family. Do some research on your name. It is an important part of who you are!

My name means:

I was given this name because:

Do you have a middle name?______________________________

If yes, what is it?______________________________________

If you don't have a middle name, you can choose one! Maybe there's a name that holds meaning for you. For example, if you study French, you might like the name Claire because it means "light" or "clear." Maybe you think the names Paisley and Channing are intriguing. Or you can change your middle name. Mine began with the letter R, and I never liked it, so I chose Rachel, which was the name of one of my great-grandmothers.

You can pick a middle name and try it on for a while. See how it feels to write it in your signature. You don't have to tell anyone until you're sure. When you're older, you can think about adding it to your passport or birth certificate. (It's a bit of a hassle, so you might simply use it informally instead.) My new middle name is:____________________________________

Do you have a nickname?__________________________________

If yes, what is it?______________________________________

If no, do you want one?__________________________________

If yes, which name would you choose?____________________

When I was your age, I called myself Sam. I wrote it on my softball glove. I wanted my parents to call me that. I just felt like Sam. It's fun to take on a new nickname just to try it out. These days, my nickname is Forrest because I love trees and think that name is cool.

What is your last name?

It's your connection to your family. Your ancestors. Your history. What does your name mean? For example, if your last name is O'Rourke, it means "Of Rourke," an area in Ireland. If your last name is Abadi, it means you're part of a tribe called Abbad. In Arabic, the word means "eternal" or "endless." The name Lieber is German and means "beloved" or "dear"!

My last name means:

You can practice writing your name. And then practice your signature below. You never know! If you become famous, you'll be writing your signature a lot.

Fun Projects

Make a name clothesline: You'll need index cards cut in half, crayons, colored pencils or markers, string, and clothespins. Write each letter of your name on a card. You can add a word that describes you. For example, if your name is Maya, you can write:

- **M**agical
- **A**mazing
- **Y**es to saving dolphins
- **A**lways wants to have fun

Decorate each card. Use the clothespins to pin each card onto the string. You can then hang up the line on the wall.

Make a name collage: Cut out the letters of your name from a magazine or newspaper. Then glue them on photos and drawings that describe you.

Make a coat of arms for your family name: A coat of arms is a symbol that families sometimes used in the past. This tradition dates back more than eight hundred years. Invent your own family's coat of arms. You can be creative! You can sketch it here:

Your Likes and Dislikes

Everyone has things they like and things they really don't. That's what makes us special and sets us apart from the rest. It's good to get to know your preferences. For example, you probably like popcorn and hate the smell of your brother's farts!

Things you might say you like:	Things you might say you don't like:
Sunsets	The alarm clock
Letting snowflakes fall on my tongue—or raindrops in the springtime	When kids are mean to each other
Meeting people from different places	Homework
Getting cozy under my blanket	People who don't smile back at me
Trying to grow vegetables	My dog's wet, smelly fur
Playing the harmonica	Getting a bad haircut
Dancing to my favorite songs	Cleaning my room
My little sister when she's not annoying	When my sibling borrows my bicycle without asking
Going to the movie theater with friends	Racism

Fun Activity

List ten things you like.

1. ....
2. ....
3. ....
4. ....
5. ....
6. ....
7. ....
8. ....
9. ....
10. ....

List ten things you don't like.

1. ....
2. ....
3. ....
4. ....
5. ....
6. ....

7. ____________________

8. ____________________

9. ____________________

10. ____________________

Writing down what you like and don't like is a way to get to know yourself. And it's only when we know ourselves that we can love who we are!

Stars

What is your zodiac sign? ____________________

Not everyone believes that your exact birth date and time can determine your personality. But think about it! Our bodies are made up of the same materials as the stars. We have oxygen, carbon, hydrogen, nitrogen, a bit of calcium for our bones, and a few more elements inside us. So, it's definitely possible that the sun, moon, planets, and stars might have an influence on us.

We're part of the universe and part of nature. Our moods can change depending on what we see and smell and hear outside. You might feel calm when you see a full moon, or you might want to howl like a werewolf. Looking at all the stars in the sky might make you feel all alone, or you might feel full of curiosity and wonder.

Weather

What kind of weather do you like?____________________

Do you feel happy when the sun is shining?____________________

Do you get sort of blue or sad on gray, rainy days?____________________

You might think about how the moon, sun, stars, and weather change how you feel.

If you do find you get depressed on a rainy day, here are some things you can do:

- If it's warm enough to be outside, you can put on galoshes and splash through the puddles.
- You can take an umbrella and go for a walk.
- If you can't go outside, you can turn on all the lights and try dancing to upbeat music to cheer up.
- You can take a very hot shower, steam up the room, and pretend you're in a rainforest.
- You and a friend can volunteer to visit a nearby nursing home. There's always an elderly person who's lonely and would love a visit.

Can you write down three things you can do when you're feeling depressed?

1.____

2.____

3.____

Fun Project

Be like a scientist and do an experiment. On the next page is a blank monthly calendar for you to keep track of the weather and your mood each day. You can even write in the phases of the moon. You might be surprised at what you discover. Can you see if you feel better on sunny days? When it is hot? Cold? Cloudy?

Sunday	Monday	Tuesday	Wednesday	Thursday	Friday	Saturday

Things to Think About

Here are some more questions for you to answer to find out who you are:

- What sports do you like playing or watching? ---

- Who's your favorite singer?------------------------------
- What music do you enjoy?-------------------------------
- What are your top three favorite books?

- What's your ideal trip?--
- What's your favorite weird food combination?

- What's your earliest memory?

- If you could be an animal, what would you be? ---

You can have fun thinking about questions to ask yourself and your friends.

You can also play the "Would You Rather?" game. Here are some questions:

- Would you rather ride in a hot air balloon or a raft down rapids?

- Would you rather see a giraffe or a polar bear in the wild?

Fun Activity

You can write down "Would You Rather?" and other questions and then put them in a basket. Then you can pick them out and answer them with a family member or friend. Or, you can make it into a game; if the other person guesses your answer, they get a point.

Take the time to get to know yourself. That's the start of your loving yourself adventure! And love for yourself is the best kind of love there is.

It's Your Diary: Write, Draw, Doodle, or Squiggle

A diary is the best way to get to know yourself. It's where you can write down what you're thinking and feeling. It's where you can be honest.

It's your secret place that's just yours, just "me, myself and I."

You don't even have to use words. Some girls draw or doodle. Other girls scribble down random words, thoughts, and feelings.

Don't worry about grammar or spelling. Your diary isn't homework. You're not writing for a good grade. You don't have to use your vocabulary words. Nobody is checking your opening sentence or whether you write slowly, quickly, carefully, or sloppily. You're writing just for *you*.

There are no rules for what kind of diary to have. You can buy a journal that says JOURNAL on the front, or you might use a plain school notebook. You can decide to write every day or whenever you feel like it. You might decide to save your diary, or maybe you'll want to throw it out or recycle it when you're done.

Your journal is for your eyes alone. It's important to be honest with yourself and have a private place to express all your emotions, letting them out of your system so you can be free of them and feel better. That's the purpose of a diary! It's where you can toss out all your emotions. After you've written out your feelings, you can see them more clearly. Then you can talk things over with someone you trust.

Keeping a diary is a way to connect to yourself. It's a way to see (and release) what you're feeling. You can write in big letters: I HATE THIS. Or in small letters: I am so, so scared. Then again, you might say, ***I FEEL SO, SO HAPPY!!!!***

There are no rules about writing in your diary. Except, perhaps, for one. You need to find somewhere safe to keep it so nobody else can see it. This is especially true if you're writing with honesty. You want to write what you really feel, but you also don't want to hurt people by what you write about them.

Words have power. Use them wisely and be careful not to turn them into weapons, because they can be very damaging to others.

Here are a few tips:

- Keep your diary somewhere safe and for your eyes only.
- Change your hiding place often.
- If you write something that's really awful, consider ripping up the paper and throwing it away.
- If something is bothering you after you've written it down and got it out, talk about it with a trusted friend or guardian.

Things to Think About

Do you have a diary? Do you want to get one? If you've already started a diary, how do you feel when you write in it?

Birth Order

Are you an older sister, middle sister, youngest child or an only child?

Does it matter?

Experts believe that where you are in a family can impact your personality, behavior, and relationships. It's something that can't be changed, obviously, but awareness can help you understand yourself better.

Are you a firstborn child? Here are some traits that might be true about you:

- You often take on the role of a caretaker and a leader.
- You might be expected to be a role model for your siblings.
- Your parents might expect you to be responsible and mature.
- You might be a perfectionist.
- You might think you have to do well in school to please your parents and meet their expectations.

The good news: You might develop strong leadership skills from your experience.

Are you a middle child? Here are some traits that might be true about you:

- You might be labeled the "sandwich child."
- You might deliberately try not to follow in the footsteps of your older sibling.
- You might feel overlooked because your parents might be focused on the needs of your younger siblings.
- You might feel like you don't get enough attention.

- You might feel caught in the middle and have to negotiate fights between your older and younger siblings.

The good news: You can develop strong interpersonal skills. You might become a good negotiator. Maybe even a diplomat!

Are you the youngest? Here are some traits that might be true about you:

- You're considered the "baby" of the family.
- You might develop the feeling that you have to be cute or funny.
- You need attention. (Don't we all?)
- You have a hard time carving out your own identity.
- You're always being compared to your older siblings.

The good news: You've gained a lot of self-confidence. You know what you want—and you usually get it.

Are you an only child? Here are some traits that might be true about you:

- You're used to being with adults, so some might call you a "little adult."
- You might have a hard time compromising.
- It might be hard for you to develop strong personal connections with kids your age.
- You might have a hard time sharing.

The good news: You like your own company and know how to entertain yourself.

Birth order may be one factor that makes you, *you*. And here's the best news! A researcher named Julia Rohrer studied more than 20,000 adults and found that birth order didn't influence their personality. So, wherever you are in your family, in the long run, it might not really matter.

Things to Think About

What position are you in your family?

I am ______________________________

How do you think it impacts you? Why?

____

____

____

Roles in the Family

Birth order in your family is something you can't change. But there is something else that might affect your personality and behavior. That's the role you might play in your family. It doesn't necessarily depend on whether you're the oldest or youngest child. We play all kinds of different roles throughout our lifetimes, when we're with different groups of people and in different places (such as at school or on a team). Your role is how others see you and how you see yourself.

The most difficult role is what's called the family "scapegoat." A scapegoat is the child who often gets blamed for problems in the family. Scapegoats get into more trouble than their siblings. They get a lot of attention—but it's negative attention. They're punished more than their siblings and feel like they're never good enough.

On the other end, there's the family hero. They try to be perfect and do well in everything. They feel they can never admit it when they're having a hard time.

Then there's the family mascot. The mascot is the comedian. When they witness their parents or siblings having an argument, the mascot tells jokes or funny stories. They might even sing, dance, or play a musical instrument to cut the tension.

Another role is the caretaker. They take care of others. If their mother or father is sick, they help them the most. They say, "I'm okay," even if they're not because they know there's someone else in the family who has it worse.

Having a role in your family means you belong! You're important. But sometimes, this role can become difficult. Getting to know yourself means being honest about your feelings. If you think you have a role in your family that's becoming too much, you can speak to a teacher, a school nurse, or an adult you trust and find ways to change this role.

Things to Think About

What is your role in your family?

Do you like your role? --

Is there something you think you can do differently?

Art Project

Make a drawing of yourself with the members of your family. You might want to include the roles.

02

Take Care of Yourself

"Remember to take care of yourself. It's like giving yourself a warm, big, gentle hug, from you and to you! It's the best way to feel self-love!"

— CLAUDIA MORELLI

This is an exciting part of your life. Each day, you discover new things about the world and about yourself. As you grow, you'll learn more about how to take care of yourself, from your teeth to your skin, hair, and more. Here are more tips to help you be the best you can be. Self-care helps you glow from the inside out!

Hygiene means keeping yourself clean. Of course, sometimes you want to bicycle in the rain or play soccer in a muddy field, and after all that fun, you'll need to clean yourself up!

To keep your body healthy and help you feel good about yourself, you need to practice personal hygiene. You already know some of these things. You wash your hands, for example, to stop the spread of germs. (Think of all the things you touched, from your sneakers to the toilet.) You bathe or shower, and you clean and cut your nails. (No biting, please!) Here are some other things you should know about hygiene. We'll start with oral hygiene. That means taking care of your teeth, gums, and mouth.

Truth on the Tooth

Yep, you already know that brushing your teeth keeps them healthy. When you brush every day, your breath smells nice and your smile stays bright!

It's recommended that you brush your teeth for two minutes two times a day—when you wake up and before you go to sleep. You can remember it simply as 2 × 2. In the morning, you might want to wait to brush your teeth until after you drink orange juice so the juice doesn't taste bitter. It doesn't matter when you brush as long as you get it done!

Cleaning your teeth helps prevent cavities. A cavity is a hole in the enamel of your teeth. Unfortunately, a cavity doesn't just go away on its own. You'll know you have a cavity when you eat something hot, cold, or sugary, and all of a sudden, you feel a pain in your tooth. It hurts! You need to go to a dentist to have the cavity filled. If not, it will get bigger and bigger and eventually make your entire tooth rotten. And then it will have to be pulled out, which is no fun at all.

There are areas between your teeth that your toothbrush can't reach. And those areas might develop plaque, which is a sticky sort of bacteria (germs) that can cause tooth decay. So, if you want to have strong, healthy teeth, it's also important to floss each day. Most girls floss in the evening, after they brush their teeth. They use a dental floss pick or string. It doesn't matter if you do it before or after you brush your teeth.

It's a good idea to change your toothbrush every few months, or sooner if you see that the bristles are becoming worn out. Dentists say a soft bristle is the best for your teeth because scrubbing too hard can damage your gums, and your gums are the cement needed to hold your teeth in your mouth.

Teeth are the tools you need to eat and even talk properly. Just try to say the word *the* without your tongue touching the bottom of your top teeth. It is recommended that you have regular check-ups at the dentist so you can take tip-top care of your teeth.

Think of your teeth as fitting together like pieces in a puzzle. When your bottom and top teeth don't match or meet in the right spots, it might be difficult to chew. Or, if your teeth overlap, they might rub against each other and make you uncomfortable. If that's the case, you might need to get braces. Here are four signs to look out for:

1. Your teeth might be too crowded in your mouth! There's too many teeth and not enough room.
2. Your teeth are crooked, going in different directions, or not growing properly.
3. You have difficulty chewing or biting into food. That might mean your teeth need to be adjusted.
4. You often bite your inner gums or tongue accidentally because your teeth are scraping them.

There's one other sign to look out for. If you feel you have a crooked smile or a gap between your front teeth, you might be embarrassed. If so, talk to a parent or guardian. You can ask them to make an appointment to visit an orthodontist, which is a doctor who specializes in braces. The orthodontist will examine your teeth and determine if they need help to grow straight or if you need to make room in your mouth. A professional will tell you if braces are right for you, and they'll explain the treatment and what you can expect.

Not everyone needs braces; you and your guardians might decide not to get them because of financial or other reasons. Having crooked teeth or a gap between your front teeth makes you special. And your smile is always unique!

How Often Did Rapunzel Wash Her Hair?

In the fairy tale, Rapunzel had very, very long hair. It was so long that she used to let it hang out the window so the prince could climb up it like a ladder and visit her.

Since her hair was so long, the top of it might have been different from the bottom. Sebaceous glands—which is a fancy way of saying oil glands—are found only in your scalp. These glands make the oil that moisturizes your hair. Chances are, because Rapunzel's hair was so long, it was probably dry on the ends. What shampoo did she use?

We'll never know! As for you, find a shampoo you like. Does it clean your hair? Does it smell good? Almost all shampoos—from the fanciest Australian ones to the least expensive ones—share the same first ingredient. Do you know what that is?

Water!

If you don't believe me, go check so you can choose a shampoo that you feel makes your hair feel clean.

How often should you wash your hair? Rapunzel probably washed hers often, especially if the prince was climbing up it and getting it dirty with his muddy boots!

If you have tight curls, you won't have to wash your hair as frequently. It also depends on where you live. If you live in Louisiana, let's say, where it's hot, you'll probably want to wash your hair more often than a girl who lives in Alaska, where it's very cold.

Most experts say you don't need to wash your hair after every sports practice. You can wash it on your own schedule based on what kind of hair you have and what you do. Girls who swim in chlorine pools usually wash their hair afterward to get the chemicals out. The same goes for girls who swim in the ocean, which contains salt water. Salt isn't healthy for your hair, so it's better to rinse it out.

What About Split Ends?

Rapunzel probably had them, too. A split end is usually found at the end of a strand of hair, but sometimes it can be in the middle of your hair, making it look like a thread that has torn.

The best way to get rid of split ends is to trim your hair on a regular basis. That keeps your hair healthy. Another remedy is to use a mild conditioner, not on the roots of your hair (which is usually oily) but on the ends. Another benefit of conditioners is that they smooth down your hair and untangle the knots, making it easier to brush and comb after you wash it.

Your Skin Is Like Wrapping Paper, Wrapping up the Greatest Gift: YOU!

Did you know that your body's largest organ is your skin? It's called the epidermis (pronounced eh-pih-dur-mus). Your skin protects your body and keeps all the parts on the inside from falling out. Your skin keeps you warm in the cold weather and cool in the heat. (When you sweat, it's your skin's built-in way to cool you off.)

Your skin does a vital job, so you need to take care of it. You can keep it clean and free of germs. Wash the dirt and grime off your face before you go to sleep.

You might have already noticed that the skin on your face is changing. You may notice your first pimple or blackhead. By the way, what's the difference between a pimple and a blackhead?

Well, pimples are caused when your hair follicles become clogged with oil. They can be swollen and red, and they sometimes hurt. They can be found on your face, neck or any other part of your body.

Blackheads don't hurt and never swell up. The skin around them looks fine. Blackheads are small and dark, and sometimes you can't even see them unless you look closely in the mirror.

Try not to pick at blackheads or pimples because you might get the area infected. Popping pimples can also leave scars. It's better to go to a professional who can treat your skin properly. A professional can also tell you what kind of skin you have (oily or dry, for example) and recommend products that are best for you.

Fun Activity

Ask a parent or guardian to help you make a natural facial mask. You'll find recipes on the Internet. You can make facial masks for your skin using ingredients such as oatmeal, avocado, turmeric, and yogurt. You can also soothe your eyes with cucumber slices.

Here Comes the Sun

Sunshine gives you vitamin D, which is a nutrient that helps develop your bones and gives you strength.

But the sun also has UV (ultraviolet) rays, which can be harmful to your skin. Have you ever been sunburned?____________________

If yes, how did it feel?

____

Your skin might feel hot or swollen, and it could hurt when you touch it. Your skin could peel or get red; if you have dark skin, that red color might look more like burgundy. A sunburn is painful, and it can also lead to skin cancer.

That's why it's recommended that you use sunscreen on your face, even on cloudy days. Look for a sunscreen with at least 15 SPF (Sun Protection Factor). You can buy it in a cream, spray, or gel.

If you're concerned about getting acne, find a sunscreen that's noncomedogenic, which is the scientific way to say it won't clog your pores. If your skin is sensitive, look for sunscreens for—you guessed it—sensitive skin. And if you don't want any perfume or scent in your sunscreen, you can buy one that's fragrance-free.

Makeup

Are you interested in experimenting with makeup? You might have already started wearing it. Or you might want to keep a natural look. All you need to remember is that with or without makeup, you're beautiful. You don't have to wear makeup to look great or have more confidence. When you feel good about your unique looks, you'll feel an inner beauty that will make you glow!

There's no one age that's right for starting to wear makeup. You might already feel ready, or you might want to wait. It's a personal choice, and it depends also on what your guardian or parent allows.

When you feel ready to try, start with something simple, like lip gloss, blush, or a light mascara for your eyelashes. (If the mascara is too heavy, you might feel like you can't keep your eyes open!)

Make sure you take off your makeup before you go to sleep so you don't clog your pores. You can use wipes or eye makeup remover to clean off that mascara. Otherwise, you'll find yourself looking like Dracula in the morning.

The Deal on Deodorant

It's important to use some kind of soap or body wash all over your skin. Wash between your toes and inside your belly button. You can use a brush, sponge, or scrubber to wash your back.

But don't use antibacterial soap to clean inside your vagina.

"Antibacterial soap kills off the bacteria that is supposed to be there," says Dr. Jacqueline Walters. She suggests cleaning only with your hand and warm water.

You can use soap on the external parts. You should clean the area going *from* your vagina to your behind. Don't wash in the opposite direction because you could bring bacteria from your behind to your vagina, which could cause infections.

Using soap on the rest of your body can prevent B.O., which is what people call body odor. It's your personal perfume, but sometimes it might get a little stinky. That's because you have bacteria living in your armpits. When you sweat, the bacteria break down the materials in your sweat. This can cause a special odor.

Body odor is perfectly natural. Each of us has our own scent. In fact, if you could bottle it, there would be billions of scents in the world!

If nobody is looking, lift up your arm and smell your armpit. You might be able to notice the scent that's all your own. Most girls don't produce a smelly body odor until they reach puberty.

Here's a little history on deodorants. Until about a hundred years ago, women rarely used deodorants! They splashed on a lot of perfume and wore cotton pads under their arms. Deodorants became popular in 1937 when an advertising campaign tried to convince women they might be smelly and not even know it! Back then, women rarely talked about things like sweat. It wasn't considered proper or polite; in fact, there was a saying that girls didn't sweat, they glowed.

Deodorants kill the bacteria that make the odor under your arms. There's also perfume in deodorants to cover up the smell. But antiperspirants block your sweat glands so you don't sweat. And sweating is good for your body. Your body uses your sweat to cool off; it's like splashing yourself with water.

You might want to use deodorant. But then again, you might not. It isn't like toothpaste or soap; it might not be necessary. Unless you're convinced that you really do have B.O., you don't *have* to use deodorant. If you do notice your smell and feel embarrassed by it, then you might consider getting deodorant.

The important thing is not to let advertisements convince you that there's something wrong with your body's natural smells. You're you. Your aroma is yours, too.

Hair...Down There (And in Other Places)

As you get older, your body goes through many changes. You're growing up, and your body produces hormones that make you get taller. In pre-puberty and puberty (which is where you are right now), these hormones also make hair grow on your legs and underarms. You might also start to see hairs growing in your pubic area.

The hair on different parts of your body might be lighter or darker than the hair on your head. Every girl's body is special. Some girls have more hair; others have less.

As you get older, you might start thinking about shaving your legs and under your arms. Again, this is a personal decision. You'll probably need to talk to your guardian before you do that. Don't be too surprised when you see your first hairs. It's all part of the adventure of growing up!

Period

No, not the period at the end of this sentence. I'm talking about the period girls get. It's a part of something called the menstrual cycle. It's the way your body prepares to have a baby someday.

Some girls start their periods at the age of eight; others don't start until they're sixteen. And lots of girls start somewhere in between. Every girl is different and there's no "normal." If you feel like you're way too young to get your period and don't want to read about it, you can skip this section. If you're curious, please read on.

You might be feeling perfectly fine. No pain or anything, nothing different. And then, *boom!* Suddenly, you might find darkish-red blood in your underpants. You might have learned about periods in school but probably didn't think it would actually happen all of a sudden, without warning. It seems like a big deal at first, but you'll get used to it.

What exactly happens when you get your period and why? Well, every month, the future home for a baby inside your body, called a uterus, gets ready. It builds up a lining of blood and tissue inside it, like a nest. But if there isn't a baby, your body doesn't need that lining anymore. That's the blood that comes out of you.

When you start to get your period each month, you may notice changes in your body and your mood. You may feel bloated or get cramps. You may feel sad, tired, angry, or confused. Your mood can swing, but that usually goes away after a few days.

You might want to keep track of the cycle of your period so you know when it might come. Most girls get their periods every 28 days or so. You can mark it on a calendar. If you have nosy siblings, you can give your period a name so nobody teases you about it. If you feel very weird because you got your period when you were young, just remember that there are other girls who feel just as weird because they still haven't gotten their period yet! Whenever you get your period is exactly when you're supposed to. Everyone is different, and there's no specific age when it should start.

There are some places around the world, like Japan, where families celebrate when a girl gets her first period. The Ojibwe, Indigenous people who belong to a tribe in Canada and the United States, hold a ritual for girls after their first period. You might not want to have a big party like the Ojibwe, but getting your period is still a reason to celebrate. You're growing up, and that's exciting.

You can do anything you want to do when you have your period. (Which also includes resting if you need to!) Once you feel comfortable with a sanitary napkin (AKA a pad), you might want to try tampons or a menstrual cup—that's an eco-friendly, reusable cup that's shaped like a bell and made from silicone. Unlike tampons, which you have to throw away, a menstrual cup can be used again and again for many years, as long as you wash it well and take it out every few hours. There are also period-proof undies on the market today, which are another wonderful eco-friendly solution. You can wear them, wash them, and wear them again and again without creating more garbage. Plus, they're comfier than disposable pads.

Remember, every girl's experience with her period is unique. You might have questions or feel a little confused at first. If you have questions about all this, it's good to talk to one of your parents or an adult you trust. There's always something new to learn about your body; that's part of the self-love adventure. This is part of growing up!

Things to Think About

What are some things you do to take care of your body?

What are some things you might change?

How do you feel about getting your period?

I feel:---

Fun Activity

Draw a portrait of yourself here.

03

Take Care of All of You

"Your self-worth is determined by you. You don't have to depend on someone telling you who you are."

— BEYONCÉ

When you think of yourself, you can think of the different elements that make you *you*. There's your body, mind, heart, and soul. You can start to love yourself each day by taking care of these four parts.

In this chapter, you're going to read about three of them: your mind, heart, and soul. Each one needs different care. You'll read about more ways to take care of your body in Chapter 4.

Mind

Inside your skull is a weird-looking coil that looks like a cabbage! It contains many cells—more than 100 billion!—called neurons. These neurons are in your brain. They help you laugh, cry, and scratch your head.

Your mind is like a muscle, and the more you use it, the stronger it gets. And just as it's good to exercise the muscles in your body to keep them healthy and strong, it's good to exercise your brain. If your brain is strong, it will help you solve problems. You'll understand things more easily and remember information.

Even on the days you're not in school, you can strengthen your mind. Learning how to think, really *think*, is something that will help you all your life.

Here are several things you can do.

For a start, read. If you like reading, keep doing it. And if you don't like reading, you can learn to enjoy it. Why? Because reading allows you to go to faraway places while you're just sitting in your chair. Reading introduces you to new thoughts, ideas, and cultures. When you read, your mind not only *reads* the words but also *imagines* characters and places.

If reading is hard for you, then of course it isn't much fun. If you want to improve your reading, start reading books for younger children. Find cute, funny books that don't require much effort. Keep reading to increase your confidence and skills.

Another fun way to exercise your mind is to play games and do puzzles. You can try sudoku, put together a jigsaw puzzle, or play Monopoly or Rummikub.

Playing a musical instrument is another way to use your brain. Get yourself a harmonica. Learn to make music with a piano, drums, or your own vocal cords. Sing! Sing your favorite songs. Join the school chorus. It doesn't matter how you sing or play; it's just fun to make beautiful sounds.

Any time you try something new, you're keeping your mind active and healthy. You focus, think, and concentrate, and all these skills are good for you!

Things to Think About

Write down three new things you can try to exercise your brain.

1. ______________________________

2. ______________________________

3. ______________________________

Heart

"Love shook my heart, Like the wind on the mountain, Troubling the oak-trees."

—SAPPHO

Your heart is an organ—a body part—that pumps blood through your body. People also connect the heart with love. This idea has no scientific proof. But philosophers in ancient Greece believed this. As Sappho, a female poet who lived in Greece in the seventh century BCE, wrote, "Love shook my heart."

A healthy heart keeps us alive. And scientists say that the love in our hearts can also keep us healthier. And self-love is the healthiest love of all. When you love yourself, it's easier to love other people.

So, don't wait for Valentine's Day! Here's something you can do to get started on filling your heart with love. Go to the bathroom and lock the door. When nobody else can hear you, look in the mirror and say, "I love you." Researchers say you can start feeling love after you say those words.

You can start a new habit to help you feel love for yourself. Each morning, after you wash your face and gently pat it dry, look in the mirror and say, "I love you." Even if it feels strange, say it! Of course, it's nice to hear these words from our family and friends. Sometimes they can't say them for whatever reason, but you can say them to yourself.

Another way to fill your heart with love is to give hugs. Hugs also make us happy and healthy. Hug your parent or guardian. Hug your sibling. Hug a friend or a pet. You can't hug your goldfish, but you can say hello!

If you can't find someone or something to hug, say hello to the ordinary objects in your room. "Good morning, dresser," you can say because the dresser holds your clothes. "Good morning, lamp," you can say. Thank it for giving you light. It's good to appreciate everything in your life, including your ordinary things.

You can find love for people and things in your life to fill your heart. It could be a dandelion coming out through a crack in a sidewalk. Or a team of ants joining together to carry a crust of bread.

Things to Think About

Look around! Surprise yourself and find ten things you can love.

1. ....
2. ....
3. ....
4. ....
5. ....
6. ....
7. ....
8. ....
9. ....
10. ....

Who are some people you can hug?

....

Can you start the daily habit of saying, "I love you" in the mirror?

....

Soul

Where, exactly, is your soul? And what, exactly, is it? Nobody knows. Scientists have yet to prove that the soul inside us exists. And yet, you might feel connected to your soul when you're at the beach looking at the power of the ocean or when you've climbed up to a mountaintop.

Some people say the soul is that small, quiet place deep inside us. Part of loving yourself means getting to know all of you, including your soul. Here's one way you can try to find your soul or spirit.

Set your clock for two minutes. Just two minutes. Then, get quiet, close your eyes, and breathe slowly and deeply. Try not to think of anything. Just concentrate on your breaths. Breathe in deeply, and then breathe out. Each time you catch yourself thinking of something, go back to focusing on your breath. You might feel a sense of calm. That calm feeling is your soul.

One way to fill your soul is to sit quietly like that for a few minutes and try not to think of anything. Or you can listen to beautiful music. You might feel that calmness when you're in a house of worship, out in nature, or singing or saying prayers.

"My tradition teaches me that every blade of grass has its angel that bows over it and whispers, 'Grow, grow.'"

—MAYIM BIALIK

Speaking of Your Soul, What Do You Feel About God?

Obviously, you no longer believe in the tooth fairy or Santa Claus, but belief in God is different. Some girls believe in God and other girls don't. Some girls call God their Higher Power; others call God their Inner Power. You might call God Hashem, Allah, the Lord, He, She, the Great Spirit, the Universal Energy, Ganesh, the Hindu god of beginnings, or simply God. You might feel God inside you. You might imagine God like a loving parent or an angel. One girl said that when she thinks of her father, who passed away when she was little, she feels he's up there, watching her from Heaven.

It doesn't matter how you feel about God. It's your belief, your choice. You might not believe in a divine being at all. In *Are You There, God? It's Me, Margaret,* Margaret likes to talk to God, which is a way to pray. Margaret says, "My mother says God is a nice idea. He belongs to everybody."

You might want to be a space engineer when you grow up. Maybe you're inspired by Vandi Verma, who's the chief engineer for robotic operations at NASA for the space rover headed for Mars. You might have no problem trusting a scientific concept but have a hard time believing in a God concept.

Here's something to think about: energy. You might not see it, but you know it's there. So, God might be a force you can't see, but it just might be there.

There are several reasons you might decide to develop a spiritual connection.

Sometimes, for example, when you feel lonely, sad, and lost in the darkness, you can reach out to God, even if you're not sure God is listening. You might feel that someone or something bigger than you is watching over you, or maybe you feel this inside you.

Having a connection between your soul and God may give you a sense of self-confidence. You can ask for a bit of extra strength before a soccer game or a difficult conversation.

There's a beautiful story about a little girl who's holding a prayer book, but she isn't reading it. All she's doing is looking down at it, reciting the alphabet.

"What are you doing?" her mother asked. "You can't read."

"I know, but God understands my *ABC*s."

Here are some things you can do to feel that connection:

- Like Margaret in Judy Blume's novel, you can write a letter to God.
- To make writing to God even more powerful, you can write a letter as if it comes from God back to you.
- Listen to Christmas carols, even when it's July!
- Go out in nature. There's a saying that God stands for Go Out Doors. You can take a walk and notice the beauty all around you. You can look up at the stars.
- Read stories about people, like Mother Teresa, who help others.

- You can sit in a Hindu, Buddhist, or Jewish temple, a church, or a mosque. If nobody else is there, you can sit alone to feel the quiet.

There are ways to find your own path and develop a connection with the spirit of the universe. You can write to God, talk, sing, listen, or pray. You can find your own path, which might be different from the path your parents, siblings, friends, or community follow. It's very personal. You can have a special feeling inside you that feels like God. It's your own feet walking this journey.

Things to Think About

What are ways you can connect to your soul?

Can you take a few moments to write a letter to God?

Dear God,

Now, here's something different. Take a few moments to write a letter from God back to *you*.

Here's a letter that I wrote to myself from God.

Dear Deenie,

I know you're going through a tough time. I know you're scared. Everything seems very dark right now. But I am always with you. Please don't be afraid.

Love,

God

It's your turn now.

Dear____________________,

Take Care of Yourself, Part 2

Your Bedroom

Your body is your personal space. Now, let's talk about a bigger space: your bedroom.

Even if you share it with one sibling or more, even if you sleep on a couch in the living room, this is your space. It can, in some small way, reflect your personality and uniqueness.

If you're the kind of girl who hides dirty clothes under the bed, now's the time to do something different. Get an old basket, paint it, decorate it and *use* it. Then you can display it as your own creative invention and throw your clothes in there (until you're ready to start folding and putting them away). Or you can buy a plain old laundry bag, get permanent markers, write your name on it, and splash it up with color. An added bonus of putting your dirty clothes in one place is that this will also help whoever does the laundry in your house.

If you've stopped collecting stuffed animals, you can still set them up on a shelf to give your room a cozy feeling. What about posters, photos, and pictures? If you like doing artwork, hang up your art on the walls and think of your room as your own art gallery. You can ask a friend to make you something. Or you can hang up photos of your family and friends.

It's important to take care of whatever is in your room. It's *yours*. Loving who you are also means loving everything that surrounds you. You might wish you had nicer things, but for a start, try to be nice to the things you already have.

Things to Think About

What can you do to make your bedroom or sleeping area be more like *you*?

Fun Project

Sketch your room or your sleeping area as it is now:

Next, sketch your sleeping area with three changes that you can make. You can add something or take something away. You can make a change for yourself!

Make Your Bed

Do you know one of the first things soldiers learn to do in the army? Before they learn how to shoot a gun, they learn how to make their own beds!

How could that help a soldier?

They learn to make their own bed because it's theirs. It's where they sleep at night. It's like birds learning to make a nest. It's a way to feel grateful that you have a bed to sleep in.

It doesn't matter if you don't do it perfectly. You're doing something in the morning that will make you feel good in the evening. You're treating yourself nicely. And that's loving!

If you don't have your own bed and sleep in your family's car, for example, you can try to keep the car clean and cozy.

Finally, if you're physically challenged and can't make your own bed, you can contribute your positive energy and gratitude simply by thanking the person who makes it for you.

Sometimes, parents want to make your bed their way. If your mother is an interior designer who invites potential clients to tour your house, she might remake your bed, fluffing up the pillows and making sure the blanket lies perfectly on the sheets. It might bother you because it's *your* bed and you want to make it the way you like.

It's a good idea to speak to your mother and suggest a compromise. Perhaps she'll agree not to remake your bed on days when nobody tours the house. And perhaps you can make a compromise, too, to support your mother's work.

And the great thing is that when you grow up and have kids, you can let them make their beds however they want.

Things to Think About

How do you feel about making your bed?

Get Dressed So You Can Get Going

Even if you're in a hurry, dress yourself with kindness. That's loving!

Put on your clothes the way you might put a sweater on a puppy or the way you used to dress your dolls. That is, if you liked playing with dolls. Some girls never do.

Make sure your zippers are zipped and your buttons are buttoned. Make sure your clothes are as clean as possible, and that includes the clothes underneath your clothes. They might be clothes that nobody else sees, but you see them. Loving yourself means wearing clean underpants. If you don't have enough underpants, try to speak to an adult about getting some more.

Then there's the issue of a bra. When do you start wearing one? You can start wearing a bra if:

- Your chest is no longer flat.
- You start to feel self-conscious—that means very aware—of your chest all the time.
- You're wondering if people are staring at it.

Then you might want to wear a bra.

What if it's way too hard to figure out exactly how to talk to your parent or guardian about buying a bra? What if the person who takes care of you is a man and has never worn a bra in his life?

Then, take a deep breath and say it really fast. You can say, "I need to shop for something girls wear."

Chances are, your parent or guardian will get the message and agree to help you.

If you're shopping online, you'll get information on the website about what kind of bra you need and what your bra size is, which is based on the size of the shirt you wear.

If you go to a store, you can ask a salesperson to help you find a bra that's right for you. It's definitely awkward, but saleswomen will respect your privacy. And it definitely gets easier.

The first bras are sometimes called "training" bras, which is a funny name when you stop to think about it. Maybe they're called training bras because they're like training wheels on a bicycle! They get you used to wearing a bra. They're made without wires, hooks, or padding. Some grown-up women still wear them and think they're the most comfortable!

The 6 Cs on Clothes

You're probably developing your own sense of style. Go for it. Self-love means following your own style! It means wearing clothes that reflect your taste in colors and materials, not just what's fashionable at the moment. It doesn't matter what style you like as long as you like it. Be YOU! Here are the six *C*s on your clothes:

Colorful: There are so many colors to choose from. If you like bright colors, wear them! If you prefer black, brown, and gray, wear those. You can jumble them up. Mix and match colors, even the ones that don't necessarily seem like they go together. You can wear dark purple with dark green, even if your friends think you're kind of nuts!

Comfortable: Wear clothes that are cozy and comfortable. Clothes you feel comfortable in.

When I was growing up, I preferred a sporty look. But my mother wanted me to wear fashionable, more "sophisticated" clothes. There was nothing worse for me than having to wear clothes that made me feel like I was wearing a very uncomfortable costume on Halloween!

If you can relate to this, try speaking to whoever takes you shopping and express your feelings. It will save you a lot of dressing room drama!

Cold or hot: You can wear layers so that if you get hot or cold during the day, you can either take off your sweatshirt or put on your jacket. Layers are always a good idea.

Cool accessories: You can change your earrings or necklaces. You can wear a new hat or a hairband to personalize your look. Even if every girl in your class wears similar shirts and jeans, you can find accessories, like hats, scarves, and jewelry, to make an outfit look more like you.

Choices: There are so many lively patterns in clothes. You can wear polka dots, leopard print, floral patterns, and stripes and stars. You can wear all of them at the same time if you want! Or you can wear only solid colors. Being a girl means being free to choose what's right for you.

Compromise: Your parents might not be able to afford to buy you the newest clothes or even new clothes. No problem. Head for a secondhand clothing store. You'll be surprised at all the unique clothes you can find.

Vintage and secondhand clothes give you your own unique style. These clothes also have history. Just imagine the people who wore them before you.

More importantly, research shows that there are just too many clothes in the world. In fact, about 85 percent of all fabrics go to a garbage dump each year. These days, many clothes are made from polyester, which causes two to three times more carbon emissions than cotton. What's worse, polyester doesn't break down in the ocean.

So, buying secondhand clothes is good for the environment. It's one way you can reduce your carbon footprint!

Cheer You Up

Researchers from New Zealand found that if you dress differently, you can change how you feel! So if you're feeling sad, try putting on a sweatshirt with a funny saying or a smiley face! If you have a pair of jeans that gets compliments, wear them to perk up. Or put on a shirt you wore to a picnic where you had a great time to bring back fun memories.

Studies also show that wearing brighter colors could help lift your mood. Which color do you think works best as a mood changer? If you guessed yellow, you're right. Just think of sunshine, lemons, corn on the cob, bananas, sunflowers. Orange and pink are also upbeat mood boosters.

Nursery schools and amusement parks always have bright, happy colors. Even clowns wear bright colors to get you to laugh. So next time you're feeling a bit down, try changing your clothes and see what happens!

Things to Think About

What's it like for you to shop for clothes?

How do you feel about your clothes?

Is there a change you want to make? Can you do something differently?

Fun Project

Think of three new styles you want to try.

1.

2.

3.

Think of shopping in a secondhand shop, a flea market, or a different kind of store!

Remember, you've got your own style, let is shine!

Sleep

Are you so tired in school that you can hardly keep your eyes open during class? Do you get drowsy at dinner? If you aren't sick or bored, it could be that you're tired. Maybe you just need more sleep!

Studies show that girls your age need an average of nine to eleven hours of sleep each night. While you're sleeping, that's when your body is growing.

Some kids do need more sleep than others. Are you a morning person or a late-night person? If you're a morning person, you're in luck. School hours fit into your body's rhythm. For girls who feel as wide awake as owls at night, school hours are more challenging. Make sure you find a way to get to sleep earlier, even if it's difficult for you.

Here are some tools to use when you're having trouble falling asleep.

- Exercise. Yes, exercise! It might seem like it would pump you up, and it does. But exercise can also make you tired. Just make sure you don't exercise right before you want to go to sleep.

- Keep your pets out of your room. You love them because they're cuddly. They keep you company, but they might also be keeping you up or disturbing your sleep. Try sleeping with a stuffed animal instead.
- Turn off your phone. Some girls keep their phone in another room so they aren't tempted. Yes, you might miss the last text from your BFF, but studies find that your phone keeps you awake. You can charge it in the kitchen and get it in the morning.
- Read a book. Reading can relax you. Just don't choose a book filled with violence or horror that will scare you. Find something interesting and easy to read.
- Try sleeping without any lights on. In Alaska, where the sun doesn't really set the entire summer, kids have a hard time falling asleep. It isn't dark outside, and the light tricks the body into thinking it isn't really night.
- Keep your room as dark as possible. If you feel uncomfortable, keep a light on in a different room, and close the door partway. If you prefer to sleep with your lights on, you can use an eye mask. They come in many different designs. If you don't want to buy one, take a bandanna or a comfy shirt and drape it over your eyes.
- Count things. You don't have to count sheep. You can count whatever you like. Try to count backward from 50. Or count backward by multiples of 5 (50, 45, 40 ...). Or try counting forward with multiples of 4 (4, 8, 12 ...). Some girls try counting in a language they're learning in school. Others count the stores in their town. (Klump's Dry Cleaning, Loobert's Stationery Store, etc.) When

you count, your brain is busy. It isn't thinking about problems. It's active, and then it gets tired. It will soon turn off!

- Make an *ABC* gratitude list. You can start with the letter *A* and think of something that makes you happy that starts with *A*. Then go through the alphabet, including *X* (for example, you only got one *X* on a test) all the way to *Z*. Give a shout-out to zebras!
- Find at least three things that happened during the day that you're happy about. It could be that you got a 76 on a really hard math test, you had a good talk with a friend, or you didn't get mad at your sister when she was bothering you!

Then, as you lie with your head on your pillow and think of all these things you have to be thankful for, you find yourself drifting off to the coziest sleep.

And you can start the routine all over again tomorrow.

Things to Think About

Which of the above tools do you want to try to use to fall asleep at night?

Is there something you can do to improve your sleep habits?

04

Loving Your Body

"Love your body the way it is, because it's the only one you've got."

— DREW BARRYMORE

Your body is going through a lot of changes at the moment. Whether you feel it or not, your body is developing. You're evolving from a child into an adult. This is called puberty. It's exciting to change, but it's also confusing and frightening because you're not sure what's coming next!

You might be nervous about growing up and having a grown-up body. Sorry, kid, there's no way around it!

There are a lot of wonderful books out there to explain what your body goes through during puberty. I recommend you read about these changes with a parent or guardian. There are no scientific explanations in this book. Instead, you'll learn ways to take care of your body and love it! It's all yours!

Body Image

In the 1960s, there was a popular model named Twiggy. She was just how her nickname describes her: skinny as a twig. She was also very tall, and people used to joke that if she stood sideways, you'd barely see her.

Back then, a lot of girls tried to be skinny like her. Some girls even developed eating disorders and became very sick in their attempt to look like Twiggy.

Girls have so many diverse shapes, sizes, colors, and styles. But most models in advertisements, in commercials, and on fashion runways are still very thin. However, now you can see a wider variety of women's bodies in ads and on social media.

Your body is unique and special in its own way, so don't compare! There are billions of girls, and each one has a unique body, all beautiful.

Including you. Your body houses your mind, heart, and spirit, and it's important. You're responsible for it. You need to take care of it and treat it well.

Loving yourself also means loving your body. It's special in its own way. The way your body is shaped is due to the genes from your parents (and your parents' parents), as well as what you eat and how you move. There's no "normal" when it comes to the shape of your body. Each body is one of a kind.

Why not take a moment to do the following:

If you can stand up, do it. Then lift your chin and feel your feet planted on the ground. If you can't stand, then sit wherever you are and lift your chin—if you can. Feel the top of your head almost touching Heaven and your feet about to touch the earth. Breathe in from your toes up to your head and back again. Feel yourself inside your home: your body.

Just think! If you lived in China about a hundred years ago and happened to have small feet, you were considered lucky. But if you had big feet, your parents might have decided to make them smaller. How? Someone would bind your feet so tightly that your bones broke. The pain was awful! Girls' feet were so ruined that they could never walk again. Thank goodness attitudes about girls' large feet have changed!

Take pride in your body. Don't be your own worst critic. Don't body-shame yourself. Put your focus on what you do like about your body, not what you don't.

Things to Think About

What do you like about your body? Write down at least four things. Here are some examples:

- My thick eyebrows
- My brown freckles
- My dark skin
- My earlobes

1. ....
2. ....
3. ....
4. ....

Now, write down four things your body can do. Here are some examples:

- Give people high fives and hugs
- Ice skate
- Play basketball
- See the world

1. ....
2. ....
3. ....
4. ....

When you focus on feeling grateful for all your body can do, you'll feel happier and more confident being you.

Mirror, Mirror on the Wall

Feeling good on the *inside* is always more important than how you look on the *outside*. That's why it's important to always smile at yourself in every mirror you pass. Smile at yourself when you pass a window and see your reflection. Smile at yourself right before you leave the bathroom in school. Smile at yourself in the rearview mirror of the car, even if you're tired and cranky.

Why?

Smiling gives you power.

You might think you can smile only if you're happy. But studies show that smiling makes you happy! When you smile, your body increases endorphins, or good-mood hormones. These endorphins decrease your stress, so smiling helps you feel better. A study from the University of South Australia found that when you smile, the movement of your face muscles tricks your mind into feeling happier.

Frowning makes your day go worse. Smiling can make your day go better.

Things to Think About

Can you try smiling at yourself in the mirror? After you do that, give yourself some stars and exclamation points and even stickers here:

Keep Those Muscles Pumping

You're growing in so many ways. Each day, your body develops and changes. And exercise helps you as you grow. The U.S. Department of Health and Human Services found that girls should do some kind of physical activity for an hour each day. Remember that the point of exercise is *not* to lose weight. It's important to exercise to keep your body healthy and strong.

Here are other benefits to exercise:

It builds your bones and muscles: You're growing taller, and your bones and muscles need to get stronger to carry your height. Exercise helps strengthen your bones and muscles to carry your body.

It boosts your mood: Exercise helps your body, and it also helps your mind! When you exercise, your body releases those feel-good endorphins. These chemicals help you feel happier. If you're angry, let's say, you can try punching a punching bag or kickboxing. You can jump into a pool and splash. As you exercise, your body is helping you push away your bad moods.

It builds your brain: Do you want to improve your memory so you do better on tests? What about being able to concentrate more in class? Studies show that exercise increases the flow of blood to your brain. This helps your brain work better!

It keeps you healthy: Exercise keeps your body healthy. Also, if your body is in good shape, you'll heal faster when you get sick or injured.

What Kind of Exercise Should You Do?

Do anything that's fun for you. It doesn't matter what it is. You can try bicycling, walking, or jumping rope. You might want to play on a soccer or hockey team or learn to play pickleball. You can go to a rock-climbing wall, play hide-and-seek, or learn karate. The important thing is to keep moving.

It's also important to remember that you don't have to be the best at any sport you try. You can join a volleyball team, even if you're not the top player.

If you're very busy and don't have time to exercise, run for a few minutes in a room. Run up and down the stairs. Do jumping jacks to get your heart pumping. Tell your parents you'd rather walk to school than get a lift (as long as it's safe.) Walk quickly around a shopping mall. Just move!

Finding a Form of Exercise You Love

What if you don't like to exercise at all? What if all you want to do is draw or paint? Your parents might search for some kind of sport you might like, but you still say no!

Try to keep an open mind about doing a new kind of exercise. For example, you can go to a playground and find a ninja area, or try dancing. It's great to find something you love doing so you can keep doing it out of joy and excitement, all while staying healthy and fit.

Things to Think About

Can you try a new kind of exercise? Is there something you've been wanting to try? Write it down here:

Food and You

Food is the way you give your body energy. It's the fuel that helps your body grow. That's why it's important to feed your body. If you take care of your body, it can take care of you.

But studies find that too many girls are afraid to eat because they don't want to gain weight. More than half of girls aged three to six are already scared of being fat. This number jumps to 60 percent for girls your age, meaning more than half of the girls your age are afraid of being fat. With all the photos and videos of women with "perfect" bodies on social media, girls start to feel bad about their own bodies. They feel they need to diet to lose weight.

You can trust your body to tell you when to eat and when to stop. You don't have to diet. All you have to do is listen to your body.

What does that mean? Eat when you feel hungry. Stop eating when your body is full, or even a few minutes before, because it takes some time for your mind to understand that your tummy is full.

Your body's weight doesn't matter as much as your body's health. You can eat right to help your body stay healthy. Here are ten cool tips about what to eat.

1. Eat rainbow colors! Food naturally comes in beautiful colors. You can eat orange sweet potatoes, carrots, tangerines, and oranges. You can eat red, pink, or

green apples. Try purple eggplants and fire-engine red peppers.

2. Drink a lot of water. Yep, simple, fresh H2O. Don't drink energy drinks because they have a lot of caffeine and sugar. They're also addictive. That means your body will always crave them, and then it will be hard to stop drinking them. Don't drink diet soda because the fake sweeteners can harm your brain. If you want to drink soda, drink regular soda, but do so only once in a while.
3. Try to eat a variety of foods. It's tempting to eat pizza every day, but if you eat the same food all the time, you won't get the nutrition you need to stay healthy. Different vitamins and minerals are found in all kinds of foods, so try to eat an assortment.
4. Listen to your body. If you need to eat between meals, go for a snack. Always keep a snack handy for those "I gotta eat something NOW!!!" moments.
5. Don't eat out of boredom or because there's nothing else to do. If you can, get out of the kitchen. Don't be a grazer, meaning don't hang around the kitchen snacking all day. Have a routine.
6. If you're a vegetarian or vegan, make sure you eat plenty of beans, nuts, plant-based proteins, and whole grains.
7. If you're alone, don't grab a party-size bag of Cheetos or chips and stick your arm in! Fill one bowl and eat it. Then wait a few minutes before deciding if you want more.

8. Look at the label. Try not to eat food with a lot of ingredients that you can't even pronounce. Of course, you can make exceptions with candy, ice cream, and cake, but try to limit your portions. If you feel you can't stop eating, find something else to do instead.
9. Try to eat home-cooked meals rather than takeout. Home-cooked food has less salt and sugar. You'll know everything you put into your dish. Plus, you can learn how to cook, which is fun!
10. An important part of loving yourself is getting to know what's good for your body. You can experiment with foods that feel right and those that don't. That's a way to love yourself.

Things to Think About

After reading the above, what are some tips you want to try?

Don't Eat Because You Feel BAD

When you're feeling BAD—**b**ored, **a**ngry, or **d**epressed—you might want to eat. This is called "eating your feelings." But when you feel bad and eat without talking about your feelings, you might feel worse. As the saying goes, "It isn't what you're eating—it's what's eating you."

Before you open the refrigerator or the freezer, ask yourself if you're *really* hungry or if you have a case of the BADs. If you're feeling bad, find someone to talk to about what's going on, or find something else to do.

Things to Think About

Do you eat when you're feeling BAD? Yes? No? Sometimes?

What are three things you can do instead?

I can:

1. ____________________
2. ____________________
3. ____________________

Eat s-l-o-o-o-o-o-w-l-y. Try to eat slower. Studies show that people who eat fast eat more than their body needs.

Eat like you're royalty. Learn good table manners so you can be ready in case the queen and king invite you for a meal at the palace! If your family doesn't believe in table manners, you can wait and do them when you're older and on your own. It's okay; there's no rush. Here are some things to know.

- Don't lick your plate.
- Don't smell or sniff your food before you eat it when you're in public.
- Place a napkin on your lap.
- After your meal, you can place your used napkin by your plate and lay your silverware neatly across the plate. If you're in a fast-food restaurant, you can remove your tray and throw out your things.
- Learn how to use a fork, knife, and spoon. This is a good skill to have because you never know whom you'll eat with. You can watch videos that show you how.

And Then Eat with Your Fingers or Chopsticks!

People from different cultures eat differently. Learn to use chopsticks because it's fun and challenging. In Africa, India, and Pakistan, people eat with their fingers.

Things to Think About

What skills do you want to learn to improve your eating habits?

Dieting Too Much and Other Eating Problems

Eating can be fun and delicious, and it is one of the best ways to feel healthy and energetic. Eating well helps you grow, and become and stay strong.

But food can be a troublesome issue for some girls. They develop problems around eating, called eating disorders.

Other girls might have the need to be perfect in everything—how they look and what they do—which might cause them to develop eating disorders.

When some girls feel stress in school or in their family, they might use food to handle their feelings. If you're feeling upset, angry, or nervous, for example, you might reach for your favorite chocolate treat or ice cream flavor. You might think food can comfort you and make you feel a bit happier. And then you might start eating whenever you have feelings that are difficult to handle. You might eat your feelings instead of facing them.

Or you might do just the opposite. You might be a perfectionist who needs to do everything just right. You want to be perfect and look perfect. You want to stay in control of your body, so you start dieting.

On this adventure of self-love, you need to take care of yourself by eating well and finding ways to feel better when you're going through challenging times.

Here are some important things to know about three eating disorders—anorexia, binge eating, and bulimia.

Dieting

Some girls are afraid of gaining weight. Even as they grow taller in inches, they're scared when their weight also increases in pounds.

The Journal of Adolescent Health found that 81 percent of ten-year-old American children are afraid of being fat. Another study, this one from *The Journal of the American Dietetic Association,* found that almost half of all children age nine to eleven are "sometimes" or "very often" on diets. This means that the issue of being thin is on a lot of kids' minds.

When you go on a diet, it means you're trying to lose weight. While it's a smart idea to eat fewer French fries and avoid too many ice cream sundaes, a strict diet might cause the following problems:

- Your body won't get the nutrients it needs.
- You won't be able to dance, jump rope, and have fun because you won't have enough energy!
- When you're on a diet, you might not be able to stay focused because your stomach is grumbling. Your brain needs good food to help you concentrate.
- You can feel sad. When you don't eat, you might be the grumpiest person around.

Don't put yourself on a serious diet without speaking to an adult! They can help you decide if you want to see a professional, such as a nutritionist, who can tell you how much food you need to give your body.

It's good to eat all different kinds of foods and enjoy treats every now and then. If you listen to your body, it will tell you when you're hungry and should eat. And usually your body will tell you when it has enough food and you can stop eating! The most important thing is staying active and having a lot of fun. Your body is incredible, and you can take care of it!

Anorexia

It's dangerous for you if you diet, and diet, and then diet so much that you starve yourself. This is called anorexia.

Girls sometimes start to believe that others will love and accept them more if they're thin. They might feel pressure from social media, friends, and family that they need to look a certain way.

Girls with anorexia eat as little as possible. And when they don't eat enough food, they experience serious side effects. Here are some dangers that could happen:

- Sudden weight loss. This can cause you to feel very tired and weak. You don't have energy to do any activities.

- You're always cold. Anorexia can make you feel like you can never get warm, even when it's 100 degrees outside.
- Your hair falls out or grows in all the wrong places. The hair on your head might start to become brittle and fall out. What's worse, you might start growing hair on your face, neck, and back. This is called lanugo. It's far more serious than peach fuzz. Without fat and muscles, your body tries to protect itself and trap in heat. That happens because your body is trying to stay warm!
- Your body doesn't have the nutrients it needs to keep your skin soft.
- You might faint often because your body lacks iron and other vitamins. You might also feel light-headed and dizzy.
- You might break your bones easily.
- When your body doesn't get enough fuel, it just can't go. It's like a car without any gas! Your heart has to pump harder to keep you going. Your kidneys, which clean your blood and help balance your system, also have to work harder. This can be very dangerous!

Binge Eating

Don't you enjoy food that's yummy to the tummy? Most girls do! But if you're eating and eating and eating, and you just can't stop even though you feel like your belly is about to burst, then you might be doing what's called binge eating.

Binge eating is different from eating a bit too much every

now and then. This kind of eating becomes a problem when you do it on a regular basis.

Binge eaters don't just eat when they're hungry. They eat a lot of food in a very short amount of time and feel like they can't stop.

You might eat a salty or sweet snack to forget your troubles for a while. But if eating is what you immediately do to feel better, then it can become a problem.

When you binge eat, you might forget your sadness. But then afterward, you might feel even more upset, guilty, or helpless because you ate so much.

When you feel confused or sorry (and we'll talk more about feelings in Chapter 6), see if you can turn to a parent, guardian, or friend rather than opening the refrigerator or heading for McDonald's. People who love you can listen to your problems and find ways to help you feel better. They might give you a hug, invite you for a walk, or play outside with you.

When you talk to someone you trust, you're taking care of yourself and your body! You don't have to suffer alone. There are people who can help you sort things out.

Bulimia

Girls with bulimia might eat way too much, like other binge eaters, but then they try to find ways to get the food out of their body.

They might force themselves to throw up, take laxatives to go to the bathroom, or exercise too much. This causes them to get very sick, too. Here are some things that might happen:

- Throwing up too often can discolor your teeth! The acid in vomit can damage your teeth's enamel, so you lose your sparkly smile. It can also cause sores in your mouth and throat.
- When you throw up again and again, your body loses electrolytes. These are chemicals (sodium and potassium, for example) that keep the right amount of fluid in your blood vessels and organs. You need electrolytes to stay healthy!
- Your body doesn't have enough time to get the vitamins and minerals it needs if you throw up after you eat.
- Bulimia can put a lot of stress on your heart, making it harder for it to work properly.
- The esophagus (you can say it! Eh-sah-fa-gus) is the tube that connects your throat to your stomach. When you force yourself to vomit, you could tear the lining of the esophagus. It might even burst, and that means surgery in an emergency room.
- You're simply tired because your body doesn't have energy.
- Bulimia can also make you feel ashamed. You want to hide what you're doing, and it becomes a secret that's too huge to handle.

Please try to remember that you don't have to punish your body and yourself. Your body is amazing because it's yours! You can give it the nourishment it needs because if you take care of your body, it will take care of you!

Sometimes, it's hard to even admit there's a problem with eating and food. So, here are some questions to answer to help you see if you or one of your friends suffers from an eating disorder, like anorexia or bulimia. You can put a check or an *X* after the question.

- Do you force yourself to throw up after you eat? ____________
- Do you binge eat? ____________
- Have you started wearing baggy clothes to hide weight loss or gain? ____________
- Are you constantly weighing yourself? ____________
- Do you worry that you might be fat? ____________
- Are you having more trouble concentrating in school? ____________
- Have your grades gone down? ____________
- Do you faint and feel dizzy often? ____________
- Do you push yourself to exercise more than ever before? ____________
- Have you lost a lot of weight or gained a lot of weight very quickly? ____________

If you checked 'yes' to three or more of these questions, speak to an adult to get help. There's no reason for you to hurt yourself this way!

Things to Think About

Can you write down three observations about your eating habits?

1. ....

2. ....

3. ....

Self-Harm

Anorexia and bulimia are two ways girls harm themselves. There are other types of self-harm, meaning when you hurt yourself on purpose. There are very sad cases of girls (along with boys and adults) who burn or cut themselves, pull out their hair, or scratch themselves until they bleed.

There isn't just one reason why people do this, researchers say. But they believe it's because some people might feel emotional pain that's overwhelming.

If you've done this to yourself or are thinking about doing it, please talk to an adult you trust.

Your Body and Boundaries

You can give people hugs. You can hug your friends. Touching a friend, holding their hand, or having someone brush your hair can feel special. It's one way for people to show they care about you and you care about them. When you're having a bad moment, a gentle touch from someone can make you feel a bit better.

Touching yourself can also be nice. You can give yourself a hug when you're feeling happy or when you're feeling down. You might touch your private parts (you can also call them your middle parts because—you guessed it—they're right in the middle of your body). When you do that, you might feel tingly and warm inside.

You can hug or cuddle with grown-ups you trust. Those are hugs and touches that make you feel good, safe, and loved.

But nobody has the right to touch you in any way that makes you uncomfortable.

Here's an exercise you can do. Stand with your feet shoulders-width apart. Raise your arms so they're in line with your shoulders. Extend your arms. Then circle your arms. You can visualize making a hula hoop all around you. This space is your space. Nobody can get into your hula hoop space unless you let them in.

If someone touches you and then tells you, "This is our secret. Don't tell anyone," that's NOT okay. If they threaten you and say they'll hurt you if you talk about what they're doing to you, that's NOT okay. If you feel ashamed by the way someone is touching you, that's NOT okay. The secret they want you to keep inside isn't a healthy secret. It isn't like a secret about a fun surprise trip. Trust yourself. Listen to what your inner voice is telling you. And remember, it isn't your fault. You did nothing wrong.

It's scary to say no—and it's hard. But you have the right to decide who can touch you and who can't. If someone is touching you in a way that doesn't feel right, even if they tell you they love you and this is normal, try to get away from them as soon as you can. Even if they are a person you love very much, you still need to talk to someone else about this situation. Make plans never to be alone with that person again.

Be aware. Some people who act nice to you might not be totally nice. If you see a man with a cute puppy, let's say, never accept an invitation to go to the man's house to see more puppies. Don't accept an invitation to buy ice cream or candy.

And make sure you and your guardian have a secret code word. If anyone wants to take you somewhere, make sure they know that word. It could even be something funny, like *supercalifragilisticexpialidocious.*

At your age, you already know what seems right, and you have strong ideas about what feels wrong. Trust that little voice inside you that says, "No!"

Adults sometimes act in ways that might make you cringe. Or they do things to make you feel uncomfortable. Listen to yourself. Remember, you're a strong, super-cool girl on a loving yourself adventure. You're learning how to take care of your body. You can trust yourself.

Practice saying no! No. No. *No.* It's a complete sentence. Know your NO.

Things to Think About

Have you ever been in a situation where you felt uncomfortable with an adult?

Another kid?

What happened? This is your safe space to write about it:

There. You're very brave to write this down. If you feel the need to talk about what you've written, you can turn to a guardian, doctor or any other trusted adult. It's important to be honest and share what's going on.

05

How to Make Friends—and Be a Better Friend

"Friendship isn't about whom you have known the longest...it's about who came and never left your side"

— MIKAELA TIU

The best way to make friends is to be a true friend. So, what does it mean to be a true friend? Here are some qualities:

True Friend	Not so True Friend
A true friend is someone you can trust.	A not-so-true friend drops you suddenly.
A true friend keeps your secrets.	A not-so-true friend tells others your secrets.
A true friend helps you solve problems.	A not-so-true friend makes fun of you in front of other kids.
A true friend understands when you're in a bad mood.	A not-so-true friend only talks about themself.
A true friend listens to you.	A not-so-true friend doesn't care when you're upset.
A true friend makes you feel good about yourself.	A not-so-true friend makes you feel bad about yourself.

Things to Think About

Make a list of your friends.

1. ....

2. ....

3. ....

4. ....

5. ....

Are there any friends who don't really act the way a true friend should behave? Why?

....

....

Are there some things you can change in yourself to be a better friend?

....

....

So, how do you become the type of friend you would want to have?

There are many things you can do to be a true friend. That means giving your time, your attention, and your understanding. Friends help make the world a better place. Being a true friend means being loyal, discreet (that means keeping your friend's secret a secret), trustworthy (doing what you say you're going to do), and showing by your actions that you care.

One of the most important things about being a friend is learning to listen. That means listening, *really* listening, when your friend is talking to you, without being on your phone, doing your homework, or watching TV. They say human beings have two ears and one mouth because we're supposed to listen twice as much as we talk!

Sometimes it's hard to know exactly what to say when your friend shares a problem with you. Here are some situations your friend might discuss.

- My cat died.
- My mother wants me to stay home and babysit my younger sister.
- My teacher is so mean to me!

The best response, first of all, is to make sure your friends know that you heard them. You can even repeat what they just said.

- Oh no, your cat died?
- What? Your mother wants you to babysit??
- I'm sorry your teacher is so mean to you.

Then, you can say things like:

- Oof, that's awful!
- I'm sorry you have to go through this.
- What can I do for you?

Things to Think About

Think of the above situations. What would you say?

Your friend: "My cat died."

You:____________________

Your friend: "My mother wants me to stay home and babysit my younger sister."

You:____________________

Your friend: "My teacher is so mean to me!"

You: ____________________

Think of a difficulty a friend shared with you in the past. Write it here:

____

____

Do you think you said the right things?____________________

What could you say next time that might be better?

____

____

And finally, think of a problem you shared with your friend.

____

What did they say that was helpful to you?

It's wonderful to learn how to be a true friend. Here are other things you can do:

- Be kind. Help your friends, give them compliments, and be understanding. It's the same price to be nice!
- Show support. Be supportive of your friends and what they want to do. Even if you would never try out for the football team, be happy for a friend who wants to try out for the team. Tell them you believe in them and really root for them.
- Remember that differences make us unique...and different. You can be friends with people of different cultures, religions, and races. You can be friends with people who disagree with you on various issues. Having diverse friends brings out different qualities in us.
- Say what you mean, mean what you say, and don't say it meanly. You can be honest with your friends as long as you aren't mean. If your friend does something that bothers you, you can tell them without being hurtful. Then, you can listen to their response, work things out, and get even closer. Being able to work through misunderstandings makes your friendship stronger, the way a rainbow can appear after a storm.
- Make sure you do what you say you're going to do. Be the friend your friends can count on. If you say you're going to do something for a friend, do it! If you make a

plan to meet your friend at the mall at twelve o'clock, try to get there on time.

- Don't try to change your friends. You might see things about your friends that they don't see. You might think one friend has a weird father or wears clothes that aren't flattering. But it isn't your job to change them. Your friends aren't perfect. Nobody is. And the best way to be a friend is to accept them as they are.
- Your friends deserve second chances. We all make mistakes, and sometimes we mess up. The key is to believe in the goodness of your friend and be kind enough to forgive and try again. You can forgive your friends if they make a mistake! You can give your friends a second chance because you want them to give you a second chance.
- T-H-I-N-K. Before you speak, it's a good idea to take a deep breath and think. Ask yourself, is what I'm about to say **t**houghtful? **H**elpful? **I**ntelligent? **N**ice? **K**ind?

Envy

Sometimes we have a friend we're envious of. If you're in that boat, you might want to say something mean to put your friend down so that you feel better. But that doesn't help you! It's better to think of something nice to say to them. You can also ask yourself if they inspire you in any way. For example, maybe their commitment to playing the drums can encourage you to pick up an instrument as well.

Before you say something unkind, you can ask yourself if this is something you might have to apologize for later on. How will this make the other person feel? Are your words adding goodness and love to the world? If not, sometimes, the best thing you can say is nothing at all!

Things to Think About

Write down the name of a friend or friends you might feel jealous of:

Can you think of what they inspire you to do or change?

And finally, when can you use the idea of THINK?

Be the First

If you really want to have a good friend, try to be a good friend. You don't have to wait for someone to ask to spend more time with you. Ask to spend more time with them. You can reach out first. You don't have to wait!

This idea can help you become more aware of what you want. If you want your friend to make more plans with you, try making more plans with them. If you want your friend to be a better listener, you can try being a better listener yourself. If you want your friend to buy you a little gift when they go to the mall, buy them a gift first!

And don't expect your friend to read your mind to know what you might want or need. Unless you're playing a game of "guess what?" it's better to tell them what you feel!

Things to Think About

Can you think of something you can do first for a friend?

Is there information about you that you need to share with a friend?

Write down one or two friends you can share it with:

The 1% Rule

You just had an argument with your friend. You're sure you're 100% right. Then, after thinking for a while, you think maybe, just maybe, you might be 1% wrong. And even if you feel you're still 99% right, you still need to apologize for that 1%.

A lot of people (and not just girls) have a hard time admitting they're wrong. But what's so wrong about being wrong? All it means is that we're human, and we all make mistakes. Nobody is perfect! The more you say, "I was wrong," the easier it gets.

You might not like having to be the first to reach out to your friend after an argument. You might think your friend should reach out first. But it doesn't matter who reaches out first. The faster you try to solve the misunderstanding, the sooner the argument ends.

Things to Think About

Can you write down a situation when you might have been (or might be) 1% wrong?

Can you be the first one to say you're sorry?__________

If not, why not?

Have a Plan A and a Plan B

Let's say you have a friend who always cancels plans with you at the last minute. They might have good reasons: they have a big family, they need to help their parents, or they aren't allowed to go out. You get disappointed, hurt, and frustrated. What can you do?

Have a Plan A, and think about a Plan B—a backup plan in case your friend cancels.

You can't change your friends—or their families. All you can do is accept them, and then decide what you want to do. You can make a plan with an unreliable friend and have a Plan B. Or, right from the start, you can decide to make a plan with someone else.

Loving yourself means knowing what you want. You can have a Plan A and a Plan B or even a Plan S—a plan with **s**omeone else. You might not like all your choices, but you can choose one and then decide what you want to do.

Things to Think About

Think of your friends. Are they reliable? Do they cancel plans with you? Can you think of other friends you can ask? Write down a Plan A and a Plan B.

Plan A: ____________________

Plan B: ____________________

You Can't Force Someone to Like You

You might not want to stay friends with everyone—and not everyone wants to be friends with you.

It's tough when you want someone to be your friend and they don't want to be friends with you. Your feelings might be hurt. You might feel like you're not good enough.

Of course, it's disappointing. But we can't chase after people and try to get them to be our friend. We can't force people to love us or even like us! The best policy is to be with people who *do* want to be your friend. They will be your true friends.

How to Handle Bullies

There's nothing fun about bullies. They're kids who treat other kids badly. They like to tease, scare, or even hurt other kids. Here are some things to help you when there's a bully who's troubling or frightening you:

First, remember that it's perfectly normal to feel scared. But even if you're afraid of the bully, you have the right, and the power, to protect yourself.

It isn't your fault that the bully chose you to pick on. You did nothing wrong. You don't deserve this mean treatment. Make sure you understand that you're not to blame.

You have the right to stand up for yourself. That doesn't mean you should behave badly or do anything violent in return. It just means that it's your job to find ways to defend yourself.

If a bully gets in your face and threatens you, making you feel small and weak and defenseless, try to stay as calm as you can. They want you to cry or scream or act out. As hard as it is, try not to react, because that might make the situation worse.

Try to stick with friends who care about you and can help you out if the bully appears. Bullies won't bother you so much if you're in a group. Reach out to friends so you're not isolated. When you feel good about yourself, you'll feel stronger!

Fake it until you make it. You might feel really, really frightened, but try to pretend you're brave. Just like dogs can attack if they sense fear, bullies go for kids who seem to lack self-confidence. Remember that nobody deserves to be mistreated. You can, and should, find ways to protect yourself.

Things to Think About

Is there someone who is bullying you? ____________________

What is their name and what are they doing to you?

____

Write down the name of a parent, school counselor, teacher or doctor you can talk to about the bully.

____

What is one thing you can do to protect yourself?

____

Don't hesitate to ask for help if you need it. You deserve to be safe!

The F-Word

No, this isn't a four-letter word. This is a three-letter word: F-U-N.

Having fun with friends is like adding spice on your food. Fun makes you happy.

Fun doesn't mean going shopping with a friend and spending all your allowance on a pair of shoes you'll wear only once. It doesn't mean lying around and bingeing on social media for hours. (More on that later.) Fun doesn't mean making fun of other kids.

Fun could be as exciting as going ice skating or as simple as buying a package of colored pencils, a coloring book for older kids, or a pad of blank paper. You could color together, make a cartoon strip, or simply doodle.

You could have a picnic, splash through puddles, or make a funny video. You can get creative or silly or adventurous. Fun is, well, so much fun!

Things to Think About

Can you write down four fun things you'd like to do with your friends?

1. ....

2. ....

3. ....

4. ....

Finally, it's absolutely fabulous to have friends. They can fill your heart with joy, comfort and understanding. And, what's even more special and fun to think about: the friends you make now might be your friends for your entire life!

So, try to remember to be the friend you'd want to have. Don't wait for your friend's birthday or a special occasion to tell them how important they are to you!

Things to Think About

Now that you've read this chapter, can you think of new things you can do to be a better friend?

Is there someone you want to thank for being your friend?

06

Feel All Your Feelings

"Never apologize for being sensitive or emotional. Let this be a sign that you've got a big heart and aren't afraid to let others see it. Showing your emotions is a sign of strength."

— BRIGITTE NICOLE

You probably know about I.Q. It stands for intelligence quotient. It's a way to measure how you think, reason, and solve problems. Your E.Q. is your emotional intelligence. It measures how aware you are of your emotions and the emotions of others. Having a high E.Q. means you're able to talk about how you feel. It also means you know how to act when you're feeling something. For example, when two-year old kids feel angry, they might throw their toys, hit, kick, cry, or have a temper tantrum. As you grow, you learn that you can feel angry and then find appropriate ways to express it. What about other feelings? There are so many of them! Here is a list of thirty kinds of feelings.

1. Happiness
2. Sadness
3. Excitement
4. Nervousness
5. Anger
6. Joy
7. Frustration
8. Contentment
9. Fear
10. Curiosity
11. Confusion
12. Embarrassment
13. Pride
14. Loneliness
15. Hope
16. Jealousy
17. Insecurity
18. Gratitude
19. Disappointment
20. Enthusiasm
21. Boredom
22. Guilt
23. Moodiness
24. Seriousness
25. Shyness
26. Shame
27. Coziness
28. Friendliness
29. Gladness
30. Love

As an experiment, count how many of them you've experienced. Then you can see the range of your feelings. Knowing that you felt one thing or another (or two feelings all at once) means you're developing your E.Q.! And that's a sure way to get to know yourself.

Things to Think About

Can you think of other emotions you've felt? Write them down, along with when and why you might have felt them. Here's an example:

I felt shy walking into my new school.

Or:

I felt shame when my mother yelled at my father in front of my friend.

Now, it's your turn:

I felt...

I felt...

Listen to Your Body

Sometimes, you might not even know what you're feeling. But your body might hold the clue. If you get a stomachache before you go to school, you might be worried about an upcoming quiz. If your heart is beating very fast, you might be afraid. You might feel your cheeks get hot when you're embarrassed. And, obviously, that smile on your face shows that you feel happy!

Be a Detective

If you're still not sure what you're feeling, act like an investigator. Think back to get to what's called "the scene of the crime." Was it because a teacher gave you a low grade on a paper? Did someone say something mean to you? Were your parents arguing?

Once you think back to that moment, you can understand what caused you to feel this way. Then you can find someone to talk to about it or write it in your diary.

No Feeling Is Wrong—It's Just a Feeling

Feelings come and go. There are all kinds of emotions that you can feel. There's joy, anger, sadness, and fear, to name just a few. Each feeling is just that—a passing feeling.

It isn't wrong to feel angry, let's say, at people you love. It isn't wrong to feel afraid, even if other people tell you there's nothing to be afraid of.

You can also feel two different feelings at the same time. Excited and nervous, for example. Bored and depressed. Grateful and lonely.

Activity

Just for fun, when you're feeling two different feelings, you can put them together to make your own word.

Right now I'm feeling cozlonely (cozy & lonely). Or, inseconfused (insecure & confused). There's also seriomoody (serious & moody.) Inventing new words is creative, and you never know which word might catch on. Wouldn't it be funny if other kids started using it? Your new words:

Putting Feelings into Words

When you were two years old, you couldn't turn your feelings into words. If you were upset, you probably cried or sulked.

Even today, you might have a hard time saying what you feel. But other people can sense that something is going on.

"What's wrong?" your best friend might ask when you slump down into your seat in the cafeteria.

Or, if you can't stop smiling, they might say, "Wow! What good news do you want to share?"

Even if you don't share your feelings, you still wear your feelings. People can guess what you might be feeling by the expression on your face or the way you move. These are called nonverbal clues. They do get your point across! But speaking your feelings out loud with people you trust can help you feel better if you're upset. And people you love will also want to celebrate with you when you're happy.

When you're upset, try to stop and find out what's going on inside. When you can't figure out a math problem, are you frustrated? When you have nothing to do over the weekend, are you lonely? Bored? When you have a big school project that you haven't started yet, are you worried?

Label the feeling so you have a sense of it. It's like being scared of a monster in the closet. You're really convinced there's a monster in there. Then you open the door, and what do you find? There's no monster—only your clothes! When you open the door to what you're feeling, you'll be able to see things more clearly. Maybe there isn't a monster, after all. It's just your emotions.

How do you figure out what exactly you're feeling?

Here's what you can do:

Take a moment to try to go inside yourself and name what you're feeling. Ask yourself, "What am I feeling right now?"

I'm feeling ______________________________

If you say, "Jealous. Yeah, I feel envious," ask yourself why. Think hard. You might say, "Yep. I saw that Emma got a higher grade than me on a book report."

I feel like this because ______________________________

____

Just writing it down will give you a bit of release. Even your shoulders will relax when you know what the feeling is about.

Or, let's say, you don't get invited to Kirsten's sleepover, and all your other friends are going. What are you feeling right now? Give those feelings words: *angry, sad, left out, hurt?* Feelings are easier to handle when you name them. If you say them out loud, they aren't just monsters in the closet. They're real.

But you still feel left out. You feel bad. What can you do about it? You could go to Kirsten's house and barge into the party, or you could be mean and talk about her behind her back. But those aren't appropriate responses. Instead, try to find some way to take care of yourself. You could make another plan with someone else, pretend to go to a spa and give yourself a facial, or watch a movie with another friend or a family member.

Things to Think About

What can you do when you're feeling bad about something?

What are some things you can do to make yourself feel better?

I can ____

Yet it isn't always easy to figure out why you feel this way or that. Sometimes, you might just need someone who can help you figure things out.

Try saying, "Dad, I feel confused, but I'm too confused to know why I feel confused!"

When you're confused or glad or mad, find an aunt, grandparent, or friend to talk to. You'll be surprised to find that they want to hear what you've got to say.

You could say, "Dr. Elbirt, do you have time to talk to me for a minute?" or "Are you busy now? I need to talk to someone."

If you choose wisely, that other person will listen to you and hear what's going on. They might give you a hug and say, "I know how you feel. The same thing happens to me!" Or they might get you to laugh and then brainstorm for a solution. Maybe they'll help you study for a math test. Maybe you can help them set the table or pick flowers.

You're not alone! You can find someone who's safe to talk things out with. They can help you feel better.

One important thing to remember is that not everyone is safe to talk to. For example, you might not feel comfortable telling your older sister you have a crush on her friend. She might feel awkward, and you might feel embarrassed.

You can learn to pick who's good to talk to about which subjects. And you don't have to share every feeling you have with other people. You might want to write it out in your diary, too, until you find the right person and the right moment.

Things to Think About

Make a list of three people you can share your most private feelings with.

1. ....

2. ....

3. ....

Then, make a list of three other people you *might* be willing to share other feelings with.

1. ....

2. ....

3. ....

It's a start! There are people who care about you.

From Small to Huge

You might think that not talking about a problem will make it go away.

Sorry, but it won't. It's better to talk about a problem as soon as you can. If you wait for a problem to get bigger and bigger, you might feel like you're about to burst!

You can share what you're feeling in a sentence:

- "Mom, I get so angry when Jasmine takes my things without asking!"
- "I feel so shy meeting the new neighbors!"
- "I'm so worried about my science test!"

When you notice what you're feeling and put it into words, it gets easier. It's something you can practice, just like practicing to play the violin! Then you'll be ready when a serious problem comes your way. Try writing down something you could say:

Feel-O-Meter

When some girls get angry, they get really angry! In some cultures, talking loudly to the point of screaming is considered an okay way to let off steam. In other cultures, people teach girls to have a stiff upper lip and not reveal what they're feeling.

You might have very intense emotions. When you get happy, you want to jump up and down and hug the first person you see! Or you might feel calm even when you're full of joy. Your feelings could be very powerful, sort of weak, or something in the middle.

No Feeling Lasts Forever

Your feelings come and go, just like your thoughts. Studies show that people have thousands of thoughts each day! Bad feelings don't last forever, but then again, good feelings don't either. (That's a hint to enjoy those good feelings when you can!)

Most of the time, you feel one feeling, and then it passes and you feel something else. Or you feel two different emotions at once. All emotions are normal, and if you tune into what you're feeling, they can tell you more about who you are.

You don't have to feel bad for feeling bad. Some emotions are easier to handle, and some are more painful. But all sorts of emotions are normal. It's important to recognize your feelings and accept them.

During your day, you can stop for a moment and ask yourself how you feel. You might notice you're relieved after a pop quiz. Or you might feel peaceful while listening to classical music. You might catch yourself in the middle of a long weekend feeling very, very bored. Or lonely. Or, as we learned earlier, a combination platter of emotions! How are you feeling right now?

I feel:____________________

What to Do When You're Angry

Anger is like any other emotion, but sometimes it feels too hot to handle!

You have the right to feel whatever you feel. It's okay to feel angry! You might feel mad when something doesn't work out how you want, when someone doesn't behave nicely, and when you have a lot of homework and not enough time.

The challenge is what to do with your anger. If you keep it inside you and don't let it out, it might make you feel even more frustrated and upset.

When you express your anger in a healthy way—like talking about it or writing in a journal—you can understand just what it is that's making you feel this way. You'll feel a bit more in control, and this will help you make better choices about how to act. You can release that anger without hurting yourself or others.

So what can you do? After talking to someone and writing it out, here are some other things you can do:

- Take boxing, kickboxing or martial arts.
- Play soccer and kick the ball hard.
- Go for a run and pound it out.
- Circle the block a few times.
- Punch your pillow or the sofa.
- Swim and dive underwater, and try to scream.

If your guardian allows, you can have what's called an Anger Wall. Then (also, if they let you), you can take an old, chipped plate, bowl, or cup, and throw it as hard as you can against the wall. Even if you have to pick up the pieces afterward, this might help you feel better. Another thing you can throw at the Anger Wall is an egg. When it splats, it might even make you laugh.

You can also find activities that help you calm down, like singing, dancing, doing art with clay or paints, or working in the garden. This will help you focus on something positive and get your mind off what's troubling you.

Doing a physical activity will help you release your anger and feel better.

Take a moment to write down 3 things you can do when you're feeling angry.

1. ....

2. ....

3. ....

How to Get Extra Help for Your Feelings

Some emotions are so painful that you might not want to feel them. You might be so confused and troubled that you don't want to admit what you feel.

If you feel really bad day after day after day, and then you feel worse, you might want to talk to a counselor, a sibling, a parent, or another adult you trust.

It's difficult to ask for help. You might think your problem isn't that serious, and you don't want to bother people. But it's like when you don't understand a science problem and ask your teacher to explain it to you. Sometimes, to feel better, you need that extra help.

You can also offer help to a friend. If you notice that they seem very troubled but don't seem want to talk about it, you can suggest they speak to an adult. If, for example, your friend is worried that someone they love might have a problem with drinking, you can suggest they go to a self-help group like Alateen. Alateen meetings are for kids who share their experiences, strength, and hope to find ways to deal with someone else's drinking.

You can tell your friend that it's good to talk to other kids who are in similar situations. That helps other kids feel less alone, upset, or afraid. The kids in Alateen understand what everyone is going through. Someone might think they're the only one in the world with these problems, but they're not!

Things to Think About

What can you do next time you feel emotions that you think are bad or painful?

I can____

Write down the names of two grown-ups you can talk to:

____

1. ____

2. ____

Can you write down when and why you might need extra help?

____

Alcohol

Sometimes when you feel bad, you might want the pain to immediately go away. Some girls might even take drugs or alcohol to get rid of the hurt feelings inside them.

You're never too young to learn about alcohol and other drugs. It might seem too grown-up and far away to even think about, but according to the National Institute on Alcohol Abuse and Alcoholism, 16% of children ages twelve to thirteen say they drank in the past month.

There are kids who say drinking alcohol isn't only about forgetting troubles. They also say it's fun. But's it's actually very dangerous, and here's why:

Kids who drink are more likely to be victims of violent crime, be involved in alcohol-related traffic crashes, and have serious school-related problems.

What exactly is alcohol? It's made when yeast or bacteria is added to grains, fruits, or vegetables. This process is called fermentation.

You can put alcohol to good use. For example, you might use rubbing alcohol to clean a wound. But when you drink alcohol, it goes into your blood. Once inside you, it flows into your brain and spinal cord, which control your whole body.

When you drink at your age, you could hurt your brain, spinal cord, liver, and stomach. Alcohol is very unsafe for you. It's best to wait to try drinking when you're twenty-one, which is the legal age. Meanwhile, as you've seen, you can find other ways to deal with difficult emotions.

Cigarettes

Cigarettes contain tobacco, nicotine, and other poisonous chemicals. These can cause many different diseases, like head, neck, and lung cancer. The American Cancer Society reports that smoking kills more people per year than alcohol, drugs, murder, suicide, car accidents, and AIDS combined!

Your lungs are like balloons that expand to help you breathe. When you smoke, you hurt your lungs. Most girls heed the warnings and stay away from smoking cigarettes. It doesn't just make your clothes and hair smell bad. Smoking stinks!!

Vaping

Fewer girls are trying cigarettes these days. They know smoking is dangerous. But sadly, more girls are trying e-cigarettes or vape pens because they think they're "healthier." They aren't.

Vaping is breathing in on a device called a vape pen. When you breathe out, you make tiny clouds. It's like when you breathe out on a cold day and can see your breath.

Vape pens have a liquid inside them. The liquid comes in different flavors, like fruit or mint. You might think it tastes good. However, the liquid contains nicotine and other poisons (just like cigarettes) that are just as dangerous for you.

Vaping can damage your lungs and make you feel sick. It's very addictive, meaning it makes you want more and more of it, and it can become very difficult to stop doing it. If this happens, make sure you get help so you can quit as soon as possible.

Marijuana

You've probably already heard about it. Some of its nicknames are weed, grass, and reefer. Some states in America now say it's okay for adults to use marijuana. But it's still not safe for kids your age. Like alcohol, marijuana is dangerous for your growing body and brain. You don't want to get messed up with it.

Pain Relievers

Pills are medicine. They might look like candy, but they could be very dangerous. Your body is unique. A pill that makes Shane feel better might make Jane feel awful. That's why if you ever find pills, never take them.

So what do you do if someone offers you drugs or alcohol? You might be nervous telling them no because they'll call you a weirdo, a dork, or a drip. Have your answer ready!

There are different ways you can say no. Here are some examples:

Friend: "Hey, do you want to try this vape? It tastes so good!"

You: "That's okay. I'll stick to chocolate chip cookies."

Friend: "Take a sip of this drink! It will make you feel great."

You: "I feel pretty good already!"

Friend: "What, are you scared?"

You: "No way. I'm just not taking any chances."

Activity

Ask a friend or adult to practice with you. It's like putting on a play. First, you can pretend that you're offering the drugs or alcohol to them and they have to respond. Then, they can ask you the same questions. You can put on costumes to make it entertaining.

Remember, drugs and alcohol can really cause problems in your growing brain and body. Now's the time to have fun in healthy ways. That's loving yourself!

Things to Think About

Do you know any people who have tried drugs and alcohol?

How does that make you feel?

Can you think of one or two people who might have a problem with alcohol or drugs?

Accepting All Your Feelings

Your feelings are part of you. They make you special. They make you who you are.

By being aware and understanding your emotions, you learn more about yourself and what makes you tick. You learn how to love yourself even more!

When you share your feelings with others, you can build healthy, open, close friendships and relationships. You can turn to people you trust to help you understand what you need. They'll offer support, care, and comfort.

Expressing your feelings is an important part of taking care of yourself. Your feelings are one part of the self-love adventure.

Things to Think About

How can you learn more about your feelings?

I can____

What can you do when you feel uncomfortable emotions?

I can____

What are some things you learned about feelings?

07

Don't Let Fear Stop You

"Think like a queen. A queen is not afraid to fail. Failure is another stepping stone to greatness."

— OPRAH WINFREY

You've read a lot so far. You've come a long way on your adventure. You'vc learned a lot. Maybe right now, you're facing a situation that's very scary. There's something you want to do, but you're afraid to try. You have two choices. You can give up, or you can decide that you're tougher than you think and won't let fear stop you from doing what you want to do.

Fear is a natural emotion. You can't stop it from coming into your thoughts. But you can stop it from taking over. You can learn to be bigger than your fears.

Here are several tools you can use when you get scared. These will help remind you that you're braver than you think and that you'll discover the courage you never knew you had.

Loving yourself means being able to feel the fear, nudge it to the side, and then keep moving forward.

The Baby Chicks

Imagine baby chicks inside their eggs. They're all curled up and quiet. Then, they have to use muscles and beaks they've never used before to get out of the shell. You can imagine how scared they are. Here are some of their imaginary tweets:

"No way! I've never done anything like this before!"

"How am I going to ever get out of here?"

"What's even out there?"

"How will I be strong enough to crack open the shell?"

"Help! I can't do this!"

The chicks have never broken through shells. They really don't believe they can do this. They're probably very scared. But they start. They begin poking and elbowing and using their beaks to break open the shell. Then they hatch! They're born!

If you, in your own life, feel afraid of doing something, think of those little chicks. They don't wait for courage. They start to do the work and then find they're braver than they ever thought.

So, if you're faced with something that makes you scared, take a deep breath and start doing whatever it is you have to do. If you wait and wait for courage, you'll never burst out of your shell. You'll get your courage once you get started.

The Hero of Your Own Story

When you think of a hero, you might imagine Amelia Earhart flying off solo in her airplane or Rosa Parks standing up against racism just by staying in her seat on the front of the bus. But every girl is the hero of her own life story. You're a hero! You might not have to battle an evil monster, slay a dragon, or cross a moat full of alligators, but you're a hero for being you!

Remember that FEAR stands for **f**ace **e**verything **a**nd **r**each. (If you're a lion, you might say, **f**ace **e**verything **a**nd **r**oar.)

Just think of some of the scary times you've faced. Maybe you've had to:

- Move to a new town
- Start a new school
- Try out for a team
- Make new friends
- Watch your parents get divorced
- Mourn a loved one

Those are all very challenging things for anyone!

You might want to crawl back under the covers and hide in bed. But eventually, you have to get up and do what you have to do, as best you can.

Remember that even famous heroes like Amelia Earhart and Rosa Parks might have felt afraid. They didn't let it stop them. They pushed the fear aside and kept going. And so can you.

Here are some other activities you can do when you're facing fear.

Make a God Can

This idea might sound crazy, but keep an open mind while you read about it.

You can transform a little box, jar, chest, or small container into a God Can where you put your fears. (You can call it a Higher Power Can, Hashem Can, Buddha Can, Energy Can, or whatever name you want.) Write down all your worries and concerns on little slips of paper and place them in this can. It's as if you're giving your problem to some larger power of the universe to take care of.

You might write down, "Mom's new boyfriend; Mr. Hughes, the mean math teacher; earning enough money babysitting to buy some clothes ..."

You might feel a sense of relief that something bigger than you will handle your problems. After a few months, you can read over the slips of paper that you put in your God Can. You might be very surprised that some of the things you feared turned out better than you thought. And other problems got sorted out in ways you couldn't imagine.

Activity

Make your own God Can! Get a jar, a bottle, or a small container. You can decorate it how you like. Write down things you might be stressing about and put them in there. Each time you catch yourself worrying, remind yourself, "Oh yeah, that's in the God Can."

Hold Your Own Hand

In Indian religions, a mudra is a gesture you make with your hands. There are traditional mudras you can learn that can help you feel better in times of stress. A mudra is really self-talk with your hands. You can use these movements to help yourself.

You already know a sign for love—a heart, which you create with your thumbs touching and pointing down and your other fingers curled.

If you're feeling afraid, here's one mudra you can do:

Sit on the floor or a chair, as straight and tall as you can. Then turn your right palm up and move it, with your elbow bent, next to your belly. Bend your left arm and hold your hand up, almost as if you're directing traffic. Your right hand asks for help. Your left hand accepts the help. You can breathe in and out slowly. When you breathe in, imagine that you are inhaling courage. When you exhale, try to imagine that you are releasing fear.

If you're at school, here's a simple gesture you can do when you feel anxious: Simply hold your own hand. You can put the thumb of one hand into the palm of the other hand, the way babies hold their parent's finger. You can do this mudra to keep calm when you're sitting at your desk, or even when you're walking in the hall.

Things to Think About

Can you make up your own mudra that could help you? This can be your safe zone, sort of like home base. Once you find your own mudra, you can breathe deeply and feel braver. You'll be able to comfort yourself no matter what's happening all around you.

Today Just Might Be a Get-Through Day

Yesterday was fun, and today is terrible. Everything that could go wrong *is* going wrong. Today just might be a Get-Through Day. That's when you have to get through the day as best you can. Maybe you're afraid of an upcoming tryout or a test. Maybe your parents are giving you a hard time. Maybe you just had a fight with your best friend.

On a Get-Through Day, you might be dealing with:

- Arguing with your parents
- Starting a new school
- Going to the hospital

Remember that you don't just go through challenges—you *grow* through them! You'll learn something that will make you stronger and smarter. What you're experiencing today will help you another day.

Remind yourself that this won't last forever. Just because today was a Get-Through Day doesn't mean tomorrow will be, too.

Look in the mirror and remind yourself what Maya Angelou said, "No matter what happens, or how bad it seems today, life does go on, and it will be better tomorrow."

Things to Think About

What can you do during a Get-Through Day?

Be Your Own BFF

You definitely count on your BFF to help you get through tough times. But sometimes your BFF is busy and can't be there for you immediately. That's when you need to be your own best friend!

Give yourself the same encouraging, understanding, supportive words that your best friend would give you. Say the things you would tell your best friend. Look in the mirror and say:

- "You got this!"
- "You can do this!"
- "You're tougher than you think!"
- "Your courage is bigger than your fear!"

Things to Think About

What would you say if you could (and you can!) speak to yourself like your best friend?

Activity

Write down the above sentences in a variety of places. You can write them in your journal. Or you can get Post-it Notes, and write your sentences on several notes. Place them where you can see them. You can even use special markers to write them on your mirror.

Fear of Not Being Perfect

How many times have you heard this saying?

"Sugar and spice, and everything nice. That's what little girls are made of."

It's old-fashioned, but people still repeat it, and that might put pressure on you. The saying might make you believe that you always have to be nice, even if you feel perfectly not nice inside.

The fear of not being nice is connected to the fear of not being perfect. You might think you always have to be on your best behavior. You might want your parents or guardians to always approve of you. You might want to look perfect in front of your friends.

But here's the thing. If you're afraid of not being perfect, you put a lot of pressure on yourself. You might get so frightened of not doing something perfectly that you have a hard time doing it at all!

Everyone does some things well and other things not so well. You don't have to try for perfection. Instead, congratulate yourself for your efforts, for your progress, and for all the things you do! Your determination is what really matters.

Artists in Japan always leave a mistake in their artwork to show that there's no such thing as perfection. They say that a perfect world has imperfections!

If you remember that nobody and nothing is perfect, then you can stop being so angry at yourself for not doing everything perfectly or not being the best at everything. Whatever you do, just focus on doing it. You can enjoy the process, have fun, and do your best. And your best is good enough!

Things to Think About

Are you afraid of not being perfect?________________________

Can you write down two things you can do or say to remind yourself that you're perfect just as you are?

1. ______________________________

2. ______________________________

Getting through Scary Times

When your family or loved ones go through a difficult period, like divorce, moving, or losing someone you love, it's normal to feel scared. It's important for you to recognize that, along with fear, you might feel many other emotions. This is when you need to reach out and talk to someone you trust about all your feelings.

During times like this, it will help you to remember that you aren't alone. There are people in your life who can give you support, guidance, and comfort.

It might not appear this way, but a challenging time can also give you a chance to grow and get stronger. You might discover qualities about yourself you didn't know you had. You might feel a sense of resilience and come to believe that you can survive anything. You'll also learn valuable lessons you can use again. With time, life will get less scary, and you'll see that the things you thought you would never survive didn't stop you.

Your Memory Bank

When you get past the crisis—and you will get past it—store it in what's called your memory bank. That's the place in your brain where you can remember your courage. Then, when the next challenging time comes along, you can go to that memory bank and remember how, with the help of friends, family, and your very own self, you survived. And you'll get through this time, too.

You're learning to love yourself. You're learning that you're stronger than you think. You can do everything you have to do. You can push past your fear by going to your memory bank and thinking of all you've already done in your life. You've made it this far. You know you're the hero of your own life.

Things to Think About

Think of a time in your past that scared you.

How did you handle it?

How were you taken care of?

This is now in your memory bank to remind yourself that you'll be okay again!

Fun Activity

Write yourself a note here as a reminder. You can say:

You'll always be taken care of!

Or, God has your back!

Your turn:

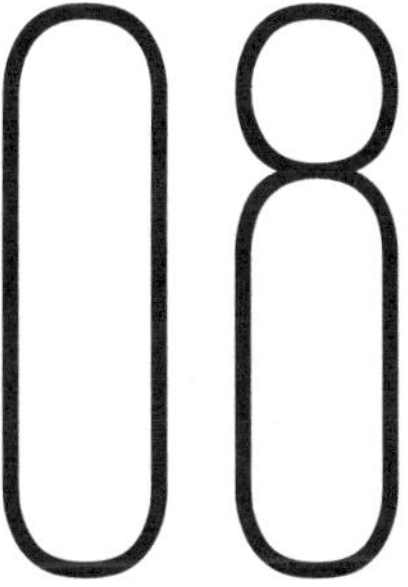

Pump up Your Confidence

"Don't say, 'I can't do this.' Say, 'I haven't been able to do this yet."

— ANONYMOUS

KEEP DOING YOUR BEST!

YOU ROCK!

YOU ARE BEAUTIFUL!

YOU CAN DO THIS!

What is confidence?

Confidence is when you still try to do the very thing that scares you. You don't even feel confident, but you do it anyway.

Confidence is taking the first step, no matter how scared you might feel. For example, if you have a dream to walk all the way from Florida to the North Pole, you still have to take that very first step.

Confidence is being you, just as you are. Unique, special, and one of a kind. You can travel all around the world, but you'll never find another you!

Get ready to believe in yourself and turn your face up to the sun. It's time to shine. You're amazing. You are. And if you don't feel it yet, here are some things you can do to build your confidence.

Boosting Your Confidence

- Act as if you're confident. There's a saying, "Fake it 'til you make it." That means that if you pretend you have confidence, you'll act braver. You might feel like you're acting in a Hollywood movie, playing the part of a confident girl. But try it. It works!
- Set a goal—something you aren't sure you'll achieve but still want to try for anyway. Let's say you dream about entering a science contest but don't think you're good enough at science. Try it anyway. It's fun to do. You can

aim to enter the contest again next year. Remember, you don't have to be the best at anything except being the best version of *you!*

- Hang around positive people. Spend time with friends who believe in you. Friends who encourage you to try new things. Don't listen to people who bring down your confidence.
- Start from where you are. If you want to learn to speak Spanish, let's say, don't get discouraged if you can barely say *gracias* or *sí*. That's two more words than no words at all. Then, when you learn eight new words, you'll already have ten more Spanish words than you knew before.
- Experiment. When you're learning to bake, you might make cookies that are as hard as rocks or a chocolate cake that looks like a mud pie. Remember to experiment and try different things. The first batch of pancakes you make will help your second batch of pancakes taste better.
- Try again. You might fall down twenty-one times trying to do a trick on your skateboard. But if you get up and try again, you might figure out the trick on your twenty-second try. You're never a failure if you get up and give it another go.

Things to Think About

How can you use some of these tools to boost your confidence?

I can____

Find Something You Like

Has this ever happened to you? You talk to a grown-up about not having confidence, and they tell you, "Find a hobby or a sport you're good at."

Believe it or not, they might be giving the wrong advice. Researchers have found that the best way to develop your confidence is to find something you like to do rather than something you're good at. Boosting your confidence includes doing things you really like that fill you with joy. It doesn't even matter that you're not good at it!

You might not be very good at making ceramic pottery. The bowls you make look sort of lopsided, the glaze isn't always smooth, and your brother says they look funny. But you love the feel of your hands in sticky, gummy clay. Keep doing it. Anything worth doing is worth doing badly.

Here are some things you might like to try:

- Start a rock band.
- Make beaded jewelry.

- Learn computer programming.
- Try 3D printing.
- Start a cleanup project in your neighborhood.
- Volunteer.
- Play a musical instrument.
- Learn to dance.
- Make a funny video using puppets and costumes. You might make it to Hollywood! You never know. But even if you don't, you're having fun now.
- Try a new sport. You might not make the team, but if you don't, you can volunteer to help the coach. That way, you can go to practices. And then you might make it the following year.

Things to Think About

Make a list of ten things you want to try to do.

1. ______________________________

2. ______________________________

3. ______________________________

4. ______________________________

5. ______________________________

6. ______________________________

7. ______________________________

8. ____________________

9. ____________________

10. ____________________

Visualize Your Success

Before you take off on a four-hundred-meter hurdle race, take a moment to be alone. Breathe in, long and deep and slow. Then close your eyes.

In your mind, picture yourself running the race. Imagine how you'll move your legs and pump your arms. Picture those moments when you go flying over the hurdle. And those moments when you feel you have no energy left. Then imagine yourself pushing forward. Running as fast as you can. Crossing the finish line first!

This is called visualization, and this method works. It's a way to have a dress rehearsal before any task. If you're stressed before giving a book report, let's say, you can do the same thing. Visualizing yourself doing what you need to do will boost your confidence.

Close your eyes and imagine you're in your classroom. Picture the teacher calling on you. See yourself walking to the front of the classroom, taking a deep breath, and letting out a smile. (A smile quickly releases tension.) Imagine giving the book report and then smiling again when you're finished.

Visualization helps you become familiar with what you're about to do. It works! And even if you don't do as well as you wanted, you still have a little more confidence.

And while you're picturing yourself in your own mind, be nice to yourself. See yourself the way you see your best friend, and the way they see you! Then you can tell yourself, "I got this. I can do this. I just need to do the best I can."

Things to Think About

Can you use visualization as a tool to help you?..................

Share Your Plan of Action with a Friend

Since it's so challenging to attempt to do something new, you can turn to a friend to share your plan for the day or the week.

You might say, "I'm going to try out for orchestra tomorrow even if I won't get in." Your friend might share, "I'm going to the library to work on my social studies project."

It's good to have someone to talk to about your plans. Once you put it out there and say what you want to do, you've already taken that first step. Then you can tell your friend what you accomplished. That boosts your confidence to keep trying. Even if you don't finish the whole task or you do less than you wanted, at least you did something.

Things to Think About

Write down the names of one or two friends you can share your plans with.

1. ____________________

2. ____________________

Procrastination Won't Get You to Your Destination

Procrastination is a very big word that means you'd rather put things off than do them right away! Everyone understands that you might want to put off taking out the garbage. But if you put it off for one day, then another day, by the third day, the garbage will be stinky!

So it's good to take the garbage out as soon as you can. As for other things, it's also good to do them and not keep waiting and waiting.

You might put things off because you're scared you won't do something well. You might have to study for a test, and you're so nervous you won't do well that you hardly study at all.

Sometimes, the longer you wait to do something, the harder it gets. Here are a few things you can do when you feel the urge to put things off.

Give yourself a reward: Tell yourself that if you clean up your room, *then* you can take a bubble bath. If you finish your homework, *then* you can watch your favorite show. Decide on a reward or treat, and give it to yourself after you do something you didn't want to do!

Beat the clock: You might drag out a chore because you think you have a lot of time to do it. But then, the next thing you know, the time runs out, and you still haven't done anything!

Set your alarm for fifteen minutes and do that thing you don't want to do for only fifteen minutes! If you're not finished yet, set the alarm for another fifteen minutes. Doing your chores or homework assignments in a small segment of time makes it easier. Having a time limit might also speed you up!

Listen to your favorite music: There's a mountain of clothes over there you have to fold, but you're dreading it. Why not put on some music? You can decide to listen to four songs and then see how far you got. Listening to good music makes any task more fun, especially if you're listening to songs you love.

You might not be able to get everything done, but at least you've gotten started. That's progress.

Pick a corner: If a guardian tells you to clean up your room, and they mean now, you might feel overwhelmed. The whole room seems like too much.

But you can build confidence by choosing just one corner and then start cleaning. You can clean just one corner. That's an accomplishment!

Have a routine: If you set up a routine, you can do a job without giving it too much thought. So, when you have to clean your bedroom, always start with that one corner and work your way around. This way, you avoid the "Oh no! I don't even know where to begin!" moment when you're faced with a mess of shirts and shoes and papers and books. You can tackle the clutter without thinking too hard about what to do first.

Things to Think About

Write down two things you usually put off until tomorrow:

1. ....

2. ....

Which tool can you use to help you do those things?

I can: ....

Stop the PLOMs

That stands for **p**oor **l**ittle **o**ld **m**e. You might be thinking of all the friends who dropped you and the teachers who gave you bad grades and the coach who didn't give you enough playing time.

You might feel dragged down by the PLOMs and lose all your energy to move ahead.

When you find yourself making lists in your head of things that are wrong, you can catch yourself. Give yourself a hug in your mind and instead, start to list all the things that are right.

So, when you blame your coach for not giving you enough playing time during a game, you can think instead about all the games you did play in. Or, when you think of a friend who stopped being your friend, remind yourself of all the friends you do have.

You can also stop the PLOMs by reminding yourself gently that life isn't always fair.

When someone once asked the great tennis player Arthur Ashe why out of all people, he got the terrible disease of AIDS, he explained that:

50,000,000 children start playing tennis

5,000,000 learn to play tennis

500,000 people learn professional tennis

50,000 come to the famous circuit

5,000 reach the Grand Slam

50 players reach Wimbledon

4 players reach the semifinals

2 reach the finals

1 wins the tournament

And, said Ashe, when he was holding the championship cup in his hand, he never asked, "Why me?" Since he didn't question the good things, he didn't want to question the bad things either.

"Why me?" is what you might ask when you feel really bad. And it's understandable when you're going through tough times. But there are things you can do to feel better!

Things to Think About

When you're feeling the PLOM's, make an ABC Gratitude List to remember all that you have to be grateful for. And that builds your confidence!

A..........

B..........

C..........

D..........

E..........

F..........

G..........

H..........

I..........

J..........

K..

L..

M..

N..

O..

P..

Q..

R..

S..

T..

U..

V..

W..

X..

Y..

Z..

What Other Kids Say About You is None of Your Business

As you grow in self-love, you'll care less about what other kids say about you. And this will definitely help your confidence. Here's a story to explain that.

There's a girl named Cinderella who wants to try out for the cheerleading squad. One of her friends tells her that cheerleading is wrong because girls cheer for boys, but boys don't cheer for girls. So, Cinderella decides not to go out for cheerleading.

Then she thinks about taking dance classes because, hey, you never know! Maybe she'll be invited to a ball. But a friend says it's boring, so she doesn't sign up.

Cinderella then decides to play on the chess team until she hears a friend say that chess is strictly for dorks.

So, what does she do?

She joins the debate team so she can learn what to say when kids tell her their opinions!

It's good to listen to other people's ideas, but it's more important to listen to yourself.

You might worry about what other kids say about you. But do what *you* like. The best way to boost your confidence is to be yourself. Kids might talk about you, but then they'll move on and talk about someone else. Follow your own dreams!

Things to Think About

What did you learn from this story?

Name two things you want to try to do, even if others might not like it.

1. ____________________

2. ____________________

All the easy tools you learned in this chapter will help you grow in self-confidence. When you find things you might like to try to do and then share your ideas with a friend, you have a better chance of doing those things. And visualizing your success will help you tackle any challenge, game, or test. Each time you take action, you can prove to yourself that you're capable of reaching so many goals. Using these tools will help you believe in yourself. Your confidence will grow, and so will your self-love!

09

Social Media Is Tricky

"The energy you'll expend focusing on someone else's life is better spent working on your own. Just be your own idol."

— SOPHIA AMORUSO

It's hard to say no to social media! It's fun. It's exciting to connect with friends who are in your area and sometimes even on the other side of the planet. On a rainy day, it gives you something to do. It's wonderful that the world has become a smaller place. But the downside is that it can be tricky. And sometimes even dangerous. So here are some things you need to remember when you're surfing social media and what you can do to stay safe.

The Downside of Social Media

Social media platforms can make you feel bad about your body and yourself. As you read in Chapter 4, seeing Photoshopped images that make other women's bodies look "perfect" can bring you down.

You might be strong, athletic, and awesome. But each time you see girls on TikTok, you might start to compare and despair. You don't like your knees. You hate your hair. You think about buying cosmetics you don't even need. You suddenly feel you have to go on a diet, even though your body feels just right.

Once you open TikTok, it can be hard to stop. Here are some things you can do:

- Set limits for yourself on your phone. Give yourself thirty minutes or five songs.
- Set your lock screen with a quote like, "DANGER AREA!" so you won't be tempted.

- Silence your notifications, even if your friends complain that it takes you a while to get back to them.
- Leave your phone in another room. You can ask a guardian to hold on to it for an hour so you can do your homework.

Write down two things you can do to help you set limits for yourself:

1. ....

2. ....

Comparing yourself to others is a challenge. But there are more serious problems you might face on social media.

Cyberbullying and Cyber-harassment

These two big words are what small-minded folks do. They bully and harass other kids online. They might post rumors about you, give out your personal information, or say hateful things about you. If you feel that someone is doing this to you, know that you're not alone. You can ask a trusted adult for help if you experience online bullying or harassment.

Trolling

Trolls claim they just want to have fun. Sometimes what they post is harmless; they're trying to be funny or get a reaction from you. But be aware that once trolls start bothering you, they'll keep it up until it's difficult to stop them. Don't engage with them. Also, most states have laws to protect kids, so you can talk to an adult about whom to contact.

Online Predators

Girls your age have to be cautious of online predators—those are people who seek out contact with girls for the wrong reasons. The FBI says that at any time of the day or night, there are 750,000 predators online!

Predators may pretend to be girls when they're actually grown men Or women! Predators find out the name of one of your friends and then say they're friends with your friend.

Predators have fake names and fake profile pictures, so you can't tell who they really are. You think you're talking to someone your age, and they might be twenty or even thirty years older!

Because you don't really know who's contacting you online, it's important to be aware of potential dangers. Remember these rules:

- Predators are nice at first. They tell you how beautiful and smart you are. They agree with everything you say to earn your trust. The creepy thing about them is that they've probably already stalked you, so they know a lot about you. They might have even stalked members of your family or your friends.

- They start by asking innocent questions. Then they gradually start asking you questions that make you uncomfortable.
- They'll invite you to meet them in a private chat room, and they'll make you feel bad when you don't want to.
- Never arrange to meet someone you don't know! Never accept an invitation like that. As in, **never ever.** Even if they threaten you. Even if they try to blackmail you.
- Reach out to a trusted adult if you feel uncomfortable. You might have made a mistake and trusted someone untrustworthy. You don't need to apologize. It happens. But make sure you reach out and tell a trusted adult what's going on.

If you have concerns about someone, you can call (800) 843-5678 or go to www.cybertipline.com.

Remember that you control your social media. Don't let social media control you. And talk to a trusted adult if you start to get that cringing feeling in your belly and feel unsure or uncomfortable.

Things to Think About

Is there someone who has contacted you on social media who makes you nervous?

Can you speak to an adult about it honestly?____________________

____

What else can you do?____

____

10

Make the World a Better Place

"Life is tough, my darling, but so are you."

— STEPHANIE BENNETT-HENRY

If you're kind and loving to yourself, you're already making the world a better place! Self-love has a ripple effect, like a stone tossed into a pond.

Your smile and positive energy are contagious. If you're happy being you, the people around you (both adults and other kids) will feel it, and they'll be happier, too. So this idea of loving yourself will spread love all around you. All it takes is one girl at a time.

In addition to loving yourself, you can do other things to help the planet. You might think that what you do can't help because you're only one girl, but think of a girl who's recently been in the news, like Jakomba Jabbie from the Gambia. When she was only sixteen, she started speaking up about girls receiving more education in science and technology. She eventually spoke at the UN about her work to help other girls. She hopes to become an aerospace engineer!

Here are some ideas of things you can do to help others:

- Volunteer at a soup kitchen.
- Adopt a pet.
- Bring clothes to a shelter for homeless people.
- Collect money for a charity.
- Help younger kids in the neighborhood with their homework.

If you start by loving and taking care of yourself, you can then help take care of the world. It's a big job, so we all have to pitch in to help!

Things to Think About

List three things you can do to help make the world a better place:

1. ______________________________

2. ______________________________

3. ______________________________

A Few Last Words

The Loving Yourself Quiz

Do you remember those questions you answered at the start of this book? You've done a lot of reading. And a lot of thinking. You've probably already used some of these tools. Now, you can answer the questions again.

- Do you have a lot of self-doubt? ______________
- Do you struggle with body image issues? ______________
- Do you often feel bad about who you are? ______________
- Are you mean to yourself? ______________
- Do you fear other kids won't like you when they find out who you really are? ______________
- Are you afraid of failing and not living up to expectations? ______________
- Do you have a hard time making decisions because you're scared other people won't like you? ______________
- Is it hard for you to feel all your feelings? ______________
- Do you get really angry at yourself for making mistakes? ______________
- Do you have a hard time just being you? ______________

What are at least four things you can now do to help yourself with some of these feelings?

1. ________________

2. ________________

3. ________________

4. ________________

And now, some questions that point you in a positive direction:

- Are you taking care of yourself better? ________
- Do you feel more confident? ________
- Are you talking to yourself like your own BFF? ________
- Are you taking care of your four elements: body, heart, mind and soul? ________
- Are you able to name more of your feelings? ________
- Are you a better friend? ________
- Can you say you love yourself more today than you did yesterday? ________

Finally, remember that you can make small changes each day. Here are ten reminders:

1. Get involved in new activities! Try new things, like joining a club or taking a class. You might be surprised at what you like.
2. Build good friendships. Be with kids who like who you are. Let them know you care about them, too.

3. Feel your feelings. Don't try to run away from them, make them go away with drugs or alcohol, or pretend they don't exist. Remember that feelings come and go.
4. Be nice to yourself. You're unique: you-nique. You're special. All kids—adults too—make mistakes. It's okay. Nobody's perfect.
5. Learn as much as you can. Each time you learn something new, you have a better understanding of yourself and the world. Ask a lot of questions! Keep asking.
6. Move your body. Your body is all yours. It's the only one you've got. Take care of it.
7. Make your bed. Tidy your room. Get dressed and get going.
8. Avoid the PLOMs (**p**oor **l**ittle **o**ld **m**e). Focus on all that you have! Make an ABC Gratitude List of things you are thankful for.
9. What other kids say about you is none of your business.
10. Each day, you get to try again. Never give up on yourself.

You'll find that all these things will pump up your confidence. You'll feel a lot more comfortable being you. You're already an incredible person just the way you are.

Today I can ______________________________

And ______________________________

It's important to remember that you can't change your entire life all at once. But you can do these things each day. Start small. Start by being nice to yourself. Making that a daily habit. And if you have moments when you make a mistake or mess up, remember that you're doing the best you can. And your best is good enough!

Aren't you proud of yourself? You did it. You read this entire book. Give yourself a super-duper enormous hug! Give yourself some gold stars and hearts and doodles:

Keep going on your loving yourself adventure!

References & Resources: Where to Turn When You've Finished This Book

First, most importantly, here's a message:

If you feel that you or someone else is in danger, call 9-1-1.

You have the right to feel safe. You don't have to suffer from physical violence.

Here are some books with further information on different subjects:

Strong Is the New Pretty, Kate T. Parker

Middle School: How to Deal, Nuts and Bolts Girls

The Ultimate Survival Guide to Being a Girl, Christina De Witte

The Confidence Code for Girls, Katty Kay and Claire Shipman

Herstory: 50 Women and Girls Who Shook Up the World, Katherine Halligan

Self-Love Revolution: Radical Body Positivity for Girls of Color, Virgie Tovar

A Smart Girl's Guide: Sports & Fitness, Therese K. Maring and Brenna Hansen

On gender:

The Gender Wheel, Maya Gonzales

It Feels Good to Be Yourself: A Book About Gender Identity, Theresa Thorn and Noah Grigni

I Am Jazz, Jessica Herthel

George, Alex Gino

Online resources:

This site has information on a variety of topics for girls: https://www.girlshealth.gov/

This site is where you can turn when you're in a crisis and need someone to talk to. It also has tips, tools, and hotline numbers: yourlifeyourvoice.org

This site has information about children and weight: http://www.bodypositive.com/childwt.htm

This is the suicide and crisis lifeline:

https://www.988lifeline.org/

This site has activities for exploring gender identity questions:

https://thesafezoneproject.com/activities/

The Boys and Girls Club of America has information on gender:

https://www.bgca.org/news-stories/2022/March/how-to-help-teens-with-gender-identity

The Trevor Project has information for young people, with a safe exit button:

https://www.thetrevorproject.org/resources/category/gender-identity/

This is the Alateen website, for kids who are in alcoholic families:

https://www.al-anon.org/newcomers/teen-corner-alateen/teen-faq/

The history of deodorant (in case you're interested):

https://www.smithsonianmag.com/history/how-advertisers-convinced-americans-they-smelled-bad-12552404/

This site has a variety of resources for you. It also shows you how to quickly get out of the site if you think you'll be in danger if you're caught reading a site for victims:

https://www.childhelphotline.org/resources-for-teens/

About the Author

Diana Rachel Bletter is a prize-winning writer and author of *The Loving Yourself Book for Women: A Practical Guide to Boost Self-Esteem, Heal Your Inner Child, and Celebrate the Woman You Are*. She has guided dozens of women and young women to love themselves more.

With a degree with honors from Cornell University, Diana Rachel Bletter has written for *The New York Times, The Wall Street Journal, Glamour, Seventeen*, and many more. She's the author of several books, including the novel *A Remarkable Kindness*.

Diana and her husband have six children, and an unofficially-adopted daughter from Ethiopia. They live by the beach. She tries not to miss a day of boogie boarding, bicycling along the shore, and seeing the sun set over the sea.

Find out more at www.dianabletter.com.

Thank you for purchasing my book. I'm happy to tell you that part of the proceeds go to ELEM, which offers inclusive, innovative programs to help at-risk girls, https://elem.org. Thank you for supporting this cause with me.

I'm extremely grateful that you invited me on your or a loved one's journey toward self-love, and I hope you found value in these pages. Please share the book with your friends and family so that they, too, can learn the joys of loving themselves. And please, leave a review online. Your feedback is always appreciated, and your support allows me to continue doing this important work—which is to help others love themselves more. So, pass on the love! Please go to https://pge.me/YeU6TK to leave a review.

Made in the USA
Thornton, CO
05/17/24 22:54:54

bca324e6-b1a7-4908-8017-e9d0e478cf72R01